QUICK AND EASY
COOKING
FOR ONE

by
Molly Perham

foulsham
LONDON . NEW YORK . TORONTO . SYDNEY

foulsham

The Publishing House, Bennetts Close,
Cippenham, Berks. SL1 5AP

ISBN   0-572-01980-7

Copyright © 1994 Molly Perham

Printed in Great Britain by
Cox & Wyman Ltd;
Reading.

Contents

INTRODUCTION

Cooking for one should be much more fun than putting a pork chop under the grill or heating a packaged ready-made meal in the microwave. With only yourself to please you can try out exciting new recipes, eat exactly what you want – and when you want it.

All very well, I hear you say, but my job or studying is so demanding that I don't have the time. The recipes in this book take no longer to prepare than the ubiquitous pork chop, and are just as easy. Many are complete meals in themselves. Nobody should expect to produce a three-course meal for themselves every night –or any night, come to that!

The key to it all is to keep your store cupboard and fridge stocked with the basics, so that you have the necessary ingredients to produce a quick and easy meal for one at any time, day or night.

SHOPPING FOR ONE

Finding time to go food shopping can be almost as difficult as finding time to cook. With a bit of planning you can do a basic shop once a week and just buy milk and bread more often. For the recipes in this book the following checklist of items will be useful. When you have used an item from your store cupboard, make a note to replace it when you do your basic shop.

Store cupboard items
Tea, coffee
Sugar, honey
Flour, cornflour
Spaghetti, pasta shapes, macaroni
Long-grain rice, noodles
Red lentils
Cooking oil (vegetable or sunflower)
Olive oil, olives
Sesame oil
Wine vinegar
Lemon juice (in plastic container or bottle)
Worcester sauce
Soy sauce
Mustard
Tomato purée
Stock cubes (beef and chicken)
Curry powder and paste

Herbs and seasonings:
Dried herbs (mixed, basil, thyme)
Salt
Black pepper, cayenne pepper
Ground ginger, ground cinnamon
Ground cumin, ground coriander
Turmeric
Paprika
Chilli powder
Garlic salt
Chinese 5-spice powder
Garam masala

Tins:
Tomatoes
Condensed soup (mushroom, tomato)
Pineapple chunks
Tuna fish
Chick peas
Red kidney beans
Borlotti and/or cannellini beans
Butter beans

Refrigerator items
These will keep for a week:
Butter, margarine
Eggs
Cheese (in clingfilm, foil or plastic container)
Parmesan cheese (in a drum)
These will only keep fresh for a couple of days:
Milk, cream, yoghurt
Ham, bacon
Fresh meat and fish
These will keep fresh for several days in the vegetable compartment:
Lettuce (iceberg keeps well)
Tomatoes, cucumber, spring onions
Peppers (green, red, yellow)
Courgettes, aubergines
Fresh herbs (in a plastic bag)

Freezer compartment items
Chicken portions
Chops
Fish
Frozen peas, beans

Vegetable rack, or cool dark cupboard
Potatoes, onions, garlic

EQUIPMENT

Depending on your circumstances, cooking facilities and equipment may be limited. The following is what you will need for preparing and cooking the meals in this book:

Large non-stick frying pan
One large and one small saucepan, with lids
Heatproof (e.g. Pyrex) dishes
Mixing bowls, large and small
Measuring jug
Scales
Metal sieve
Cheese grater
Tin opener
Bottle opener
Fish slice or spatula
Wooden spoon
Sharp chopping knife
Chopping board
Spoons –tablespoon, dessertspoon and teaspoon

MEASUREMENTS

A measuring jug and scales are high on the list of essential equipment. But if you don't own them, an ordinary mug holds ½ pint/300 ml, and you can measure fairly accurately with spoons:

Flour: 1 heaped tablespoon = 25g/1oz

Sugar: 1 slightly rounded tablespoon = 25g/1oz

Butter and margarine: 1 slightly round tablespoon = 25g/1 oz (If the butter is hard, a 2.5cm/1in cube weighs 25g/1oz.)

Cheese: 1 heaped tablespoon grated cheese = 25g/1oz

Rice: 1 slightly round tablespoon = 25g/1oz
        1 small cup = 100g/4oz

Pasta shapes: 1 handful = approx 75g/3oz

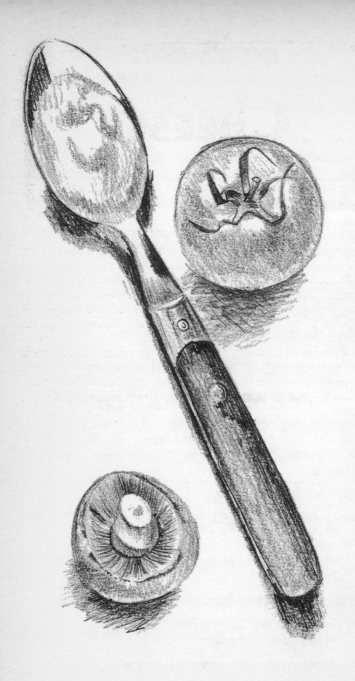

Cheese

Cheese is a very adaptable food - you can use it in cooking, either as a main ingredient, for flavouring sauces or as a topping; and it is excellent for eating as a quick snack. Because it is so rich in protein, cheese is an excellent substitute for meat in vegetarian dishes. It is also a good source of calcium and vitamin A. But slimmers beware - it is also high in fat.

Cheese will keep in the refrigerator for up to a week if wrapped in clingfilm or foil, or in a plastic container. It is therefore a good standby food - the basis of a variety of quick meals when you haven't had time to shop.

CAULIFLOWER CHEESE

ingredients	Metric	Imperial	American
Cheese sauce (see page 134)			
Cauliflower florets	150 g	6 oz	6 oz
Cheddar cheese, grated	25 g	1 oz	1 oz

method

1. Cook the cauliflower florets in a saucepan of boiling, salted water for about 15 minutes, or until soft. Drain and turn into a fireproof dish.

2. Pour over the prepared cheese sauce.

3. Sprinkle grated cheese on top and put under a hot grill for a few minutes until the top is browned.

4. Eat with some good crusty bread.

10 min Preparation time
20 min Cooking time

MACARONI CHEESE

You can add other ingredients to this basic macaroni cheese. For variety try adding some chopped ham or cooked bacon, sliced cooked mushrooms, or some slices of tomato on top.

ingredients	Metric	Imperial	American
Cheese sauce (see page 134)			
Macaroni	*75 g*	*3 oz*	*3 oz*
Cheddar cheese, grated	*25 g*	*1 oz*	*1 oz*

method

1. Cook the macaroni in a saucepan of boiling, salted water for about 10 minutes, or until soft. Drain and turn into a fireproof dish.

2. Pour over the prepared cheese sauce.

3. Sprinkle grated cheese on top and put under a hot grill for a few minutes until the top is browned.

10 min Preparation time
15 min Cooking time

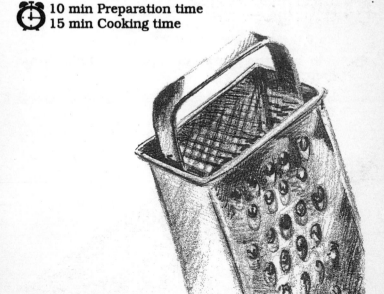

CHEESE AND POTATO PIE

If you use leftover cooked potatoes, this dish will take only 10 minutes to cook.

ingredients	Metric	Imperial	American
Potatoes	2	2	2
Butter or margarine	15 g	½ oz	½ oz
Milk	15 ml	1 tbsp	1 tbsp
Salt and pepper			
Cheddar cheese, grated	50 g	2 oz	2 oz
Tomato, sliced	1	1	1

method

1. Peel the potatoes and cut into even-sized pieces. Cook in boiling, salted water for 15-20 minutes, until soft. Drain into a sieve and then return them to the pan.

2. Mash the potatoes with a fork, then add the butter, milk, and a little salt and pepper. Beat until the potatoes are creamy.

3. Add half the grated cheese and spoon into a fireproof dish.

4. Sprinkle over the remaining cheese, then arrange the sliced tomato on top.

5. Put under a hot grill until the top is golden brown.

10 min Preparation time
30 min Cooking time

CHEESE OMELETTE

ingredients	Metric	Imperial	American
Eggs	2	2	2
Salt and pepper			
Oil	10 ml	2 tsp	2 tsp
Cheddar cheese, grated	50 g	2 oz	2 oz

method

1. Break the eggs into a basin. Add salt and pepper and a tablespoon of cold water. Beat together with a fork.

2. Heat a frying pan to a fairly high temperature and add the oil.

3. Pour in the eggs, swirling them over the bottom of the pan. As the egg sets, draw the cooked bits to the centre with a fish slice or spatula, allowing the uncooked egg to run to the sides. Tilt the pan as you work.

4. Before the omelette is completely set, spoon most of the grated cheese onto one half, and fold the other half over. Sprinkle the remaining cheese on top.

5. Slide the omelette out onto a warm plate.

6. Eat with crusty bread and a green salad.

 10 - 15 min Preparation time
10 min Cooking time

CHEESY RICE

If you have some left-over, cooked rice, this is a quick way of making a tasty supper dish.

ingredients	Metric	Imperial	American
Cooking oil	15 ml	1 tbsp	1 tbsp
Small onion, peeled and sliced	1	1	1
Bacon, chopped	50 g	2 oz	2 oz
Cooked rice	1 cup	1 cup	1 cup
Cheddar or Gruyère cheese, grated	50 g	2 oz	2 oz
Salt and pepper			

method

1. Heat the oil in a frying pan and gently cook the onion and bacon for 5 minutes.

2 . Add the rice and cheese, and season with salt and pepper.

3. Continue cooking, stirring all the time, until everything is well mixed and heated through.

4. Eat with a mixed salad.

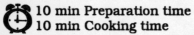 10 min Preparation time
10 min Cooking time

CHEESY NOODLES

ingredients	Metric	Imperial	American
Noodles	75-100g	3-4 oz	3-4 oz
Cheddar cheese, grated	50 g	2 oz	2 oz
Butter	25 g	1 oz	1 oz
Salt			
Black pepper			

method

1. Cook the noodles according to the instructions on the packet. Drain them and put them back into the warm saucepan.

2. Stir in the butter and grated cheese, and season with salt and pepper.

3. Eat with a side salad.

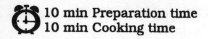 10 min Preparation time
10 min Cooking time

CROQUE MONSIEUR

This quick snack tastes best with Gruyére cheese, but Cheddar may be used as a substitute.

ingredients	Metric	Imperial	American
Slices of bread	2	2	2
Butter or margarine			
Slice of ham	1	1	1
Slice of Gruyére cheese	1	1	1
Oil for frying			

method

1. Spread the slices of bread with butter or margarine.

2. Put the ham and cheese between the slices of bread to make a sandwich.

3. Heat some oil in a frying pan and fry the sandwich until golden brown on both sides.

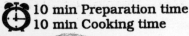 10 min Preparation time
10 min Cooking time

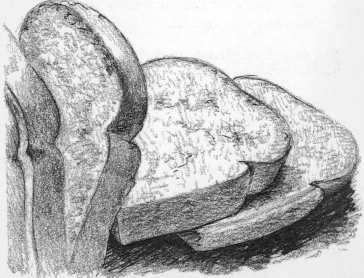

EGGS AND LEEKS
AU GRATIN

ingredients	Metric	Imperial	American
Eggs	2	2	2
Leeks	2	2	2
Butter	12.5 g	½ oz	½ oz
Cheddar cheese, grated	25 g	1 oz	1 oz
Cheese sauce (see page 134)			

method

1. Cook the eggs in boiling water for 8 minutes. Plunge into cold water and remove the shells.

2. Meanwhile clean and chop the leeks. Melt the butter in a frying pan and cook gently for 5 minutes.

3. Make the cheese sauce (page 134).

4. Put the leeks into a heatproof dish. Halve the eggs and arrange on top of the leeks, rounded side up. Pour over the cheese sauce. Sprinkle grated cheese on top.

5. Put under a hot grill until nicely browned.

6. Serve with crusty bread.

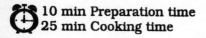 10 min Preparation time
25 min Cooking time

FRENCH BREAD OR PITTA PIZZA

Use French bread split in half lengthwise, or a pitta bread, to make a substantial snack that is a cross between cheese on toast and a pizza. Other suggested toppings are listed below.

ingredients	Metric	Imperial	American
French or pitta bread			
Tomato, sliced	1	1	1
Slices of ham	2	2	2
Slices of Cheddar cheese	4	4	4
Mixed dried herbs	5 ml	1 tsp	1 tsp

method

1. If you are using French bread, split it in half lengthwise.

2. Arrange slices of tomato, ham and cheese on both halves of the bread, or on pittas.

3. Cook under a hot grill until the cheese is brown and bubbling.

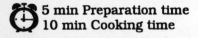 5 min Preparation time
10 min Cooking time

other suggested toppings

Mushroom, tomato and cheese: Peel and slice the mushrooms, slice the tomatoes, grate cheese on top.

Tomato, salami and cheese: Slice the tomatoes and sprinkle with salt and pepper. Arrange slices of salami and cheese on top.

Onion, sweetcorn and cheese: Peel and slice the onion into very thin rings. Spoon some drained sweetcorn over the onions. Grate cheese on top.

Chicken

Lots of tasty meals-for-one can be made from an individual chicken joint. You have a choice of breast, leg or drumsticks. Boned chicken breast is particularly convenient because it is so quick to cook, and there is no waste. Fresh chicken tastes better and is more tender than frozen. If you do buy a frozen joint you can speed up the defrosting process by holding it under cold running water. Never use hot water because germs thrive in warm conditions and chicken is prone to nasty bacteria.

For more ideas see Stir-fry (page 144) and Three Meals in One (page 156).

CHICKEN IN MUSHROOM SAUCE

ingredients	Metric	Imperial	American
Chicken joint			
Butter or margarine	12.5 g	½ oz	½ oz
Small onion, peeled and chopped	1	1	1
Tin condensed mushroom soup	½	½	½
Milk	60 ml	4 tbsp	4 tbsp
Cream	30 ml	2 tbsp	2 tbsp
Lemon juice	2.5 ml	½ tsp	½ tsp

method

1. Melt the butter and fry the chicken joint and onion until the chicken is browned all over.

2. Mix the soup and milk together and pour over the chicken.

3. Bring to the boil, cover the pan and simmer gently for 30 minutes, or until the chicken is tender.

4. Remove from the heat and stir in the lemon juice and cream before eating.

5. Serve with rice or boiled potatoes, and cooked vegetables or a salad.

10 min Preparation time
35 min Cooking time

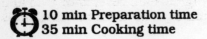

CHICKEN CREOLE

ingredients	Metric	Imperial	American
Chicken joint	1	1	1
Flour	25 g	1 oz	1 oz
Salt and pepper			
Oil	15 ml	1 tbsp	1 tbsp
Small onion, peeled and chopped	1	1	1
Green pepper, chopped	½	½	½
Tin tomatoes	200 g	7 oz	7 oz
Worcester sauce	5 ml	1 tsp	1 tsp
Vinegar	5 ml	1 tsp	1 tsp
Brown sugar	5 ml	1 tsp	1 tsp

method

1. Defrost the chicken joint if it is frozen, wipe and pat dry.

2. In a shallow dish or a plate mix the flour with a little salt and pepper.

3. Dip the chicken joint in the flour so that it is coated on all sides.

4. Heat the oil in a pan and add the chicken joint, onion and green pepper. Fry until the chicken is browned all over.

5. Add the remaining ingredients, cover with a lid and cook for about 30 minutes, or until the chicken is tender.

6. Serve with rice or boiled potatoes, and a salad.

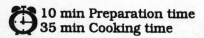
10 min Preparation time
35 min Cooking time

ONE POT CHICKEN AND POTATO

ingredients	Metric	Imperial	American
Chicken joint	1	1	1
Flour	25 g	1 oz	1 oz
Salt and pepper			
Butter or margarine	25 g	1 oz	1 oz
Small onion, peeled and chopped	1	1	1
Tomatoes, chopped	2	2	2
Large potato, peeled and diced	1	1	1
Dried herbs	2.5 ml	½ tsp	½ tsp

method

1. In a shallow dish or a plate mix the flour with a little salt and pepper.

2. Dip the chicken in the flour so that it is coated on all sides.

3. Melt the butter in a saucepan and fry the onion until it begins to soften.

4. Add the chicken and fry until golden brown on all sides.

5. Add the tomatoes, diced potato, herbs, salt and pepper.

6. Cover with a lid and simmer over a low heat for about 30 minutes, or until the chicken is tender.

7. Served with cooked vegetables or a salad.

10 min Preparation time
40 min Cooking time

CHICKEN AND RICE

ingredients	Metric	Imperial	American
Chicken joint	1	1	1
Butter or margarine	12.5 g	½ oz	½ oz
Small onion, peeled and finely chopped	1	1	1
Carrot, thinly sliced	1	1	1
Long grain rice	100 g	4 oz	4 oz
Water			
Dried mixed herbs	2.5 ml	½ tsp	½ tsp
Salt and pepper			

method

1. Melt the butter in a saucepan and gently fry the onion and carrot.

2. Add the chicken joint and brown it on all sides.

3. Add the rice and enough water to cover everything.

4. Add the herbs and season with salt and pepper.

5. Bring to the boil, then reduce the heat, cover with a lid and simmer for 40 minutes. (Check occasionally to see if it is drying up - if so, add a little extra water.)

6. Serve with a green salad.

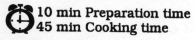
10 min Preparation time
45 min Cooking time

LEMON CHICKEN

ingredients	Metric	Imperial	American
Boned and skinned chicken breast	1	1	1
Salt and pepper			
Oil	15 ml	1 tbsp	1 tbsp
Chicken stock (made with stock cube)	15 ml	1 tbsp	1 tbsp
Lemon juice	5 ml	1 tsp	1 tsp
Soy sauce	5 ml	1 tsp	1 tsp
Spring onion, chopped	2	2	2

method

1. Cut the chicken into thin strips and season it well with salt and pepper.

2. Heat the oil in a frying pan and fry the chicken quickly, stirring all the time, until it is golden brown.

3. Add the stock, lemon juice and soy sauce.

4. Stir in the spring onions and cook for 2-3 minutes.

5. Serve with rice, and stir-fried vegetables or a salad.

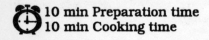
10 min Preparation time
10 min Cooking time

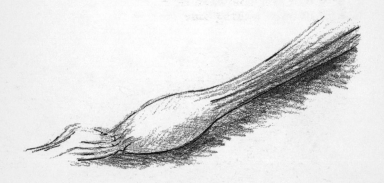

CHICKEN MARSALA

This is what you do with the remains of the bottle of marsala that you brought back from your Italian holiday.

ingredients	Metric	Imperial	American
Boned and skinned chicken breast	*1*	*1*	*1*
Oil	*15 ml*	*1 tbsp*	*1 tbsp*
Marsala	*15 ml*	*1 tbsp*	*1 tbsp*
Salt and pepper			
Cream	*15 ml*	*1 tbsp*	*1 tbsp*

method

1. Heat the oil and fry the chicken breast until browned on both sides.

2. Pour off any excess fat and add the marsala. Season with salt and pepper.

3. Cover and cook gently for 10 minutes.

4. Remove the pan from the heat and stir in the cream.

5. Put under a hot grill until golden brown.

6. Serve with rice or boiled potatoes, cooked vegetables or a salad.

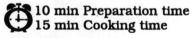 10 min Preparation time
15 min Cooking time

ITALIAN CHICKEN

ingredients	Metric	Imperial	American
Boned and skinned chicken breast	1	1	1
Oil	15 ml	1 tbsp	1 tbsp
Clove of garlic, crushed	1	1	1
Small red pepper, chopped	½	½	½
Small yellow pepper, chopped	½	½	½
Tin chopped tomatoes	200 g	7 oz	7 oz
Dried herbs	2.5 ml	½ tsp	½ tsp
Salt and pepper			

method

1. Heat the oil in a saucepan and fry the crushed garlic for 1 minute.

2. Add the chicken breast and fry until browned on both sides.

3. Add the peppers, tomatoes and herbs. Season with salt and pepper.

4. Bring everything up to simmering point, then cook, without a lid, for 15 minutes.

5. Serve with rice and a green salad.

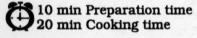 10 min Preparation time
20 min Cooking time

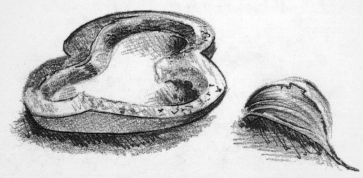

CHICKEN KEBABS

ingredients	Metric	Imperial	American
Boned and skinned chicken breast	1	1	1
Natural yoghurt	30 ml	2 tbsp	2 tbsp
Honey	15 ml	1 tbsp	1 tbsp
Clove of garlic, crushed	1	1	1
Curry paste	5 ml	1 tsp	1 tsp
Yellow pepper, cut into cubes	½	½	½
Button mushrooms	6	6	6

method

1. Cut the chicken into cubes, and put it into a bowl with the yoghurt, honey, garlic and curry paste. Mix thoroughly and leave to stand for half-an-hour if you have time.

2. Push the chicken onto a skewer alternately with yellow pepper and mushrooms.

3. Cook under a hot grill for 15 minutes, turning frequently.

4. Serve on a bed of spiced rice, with a salad.

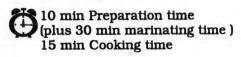 10 min Preparation time
(plus 30 min marinating time)
15 min Cooking time

Chicken Kebabs and Satay Sauce

ingredients	Metric	Imperial	American
Streaky bacon rashers	2	2	2
Banana, cut in chunks	1	1	1
Boneless chicken breast	50-75g	2-3 oz	2-3 oz
Honey	5 ml	1 tsp	1 tsp
Worcester sauce	5 ml	1 tsp	1 tsp
Lemon juice	5 ml	1 tsp	1 tsp
For satay sauce:			
Lemon juice	15 ml	1 tbsp	1 tbsp
Clove of garlic, crushed	1	1	1
Crunchy peanut butter	1 tbsp	1 tbsp	1 tbsp
Orange juice	30 ml	2 tbsp	2 tbsp
Spring onions, chopped	2	2	2
Cayenne pepper (optional)	pinch	pinch	pinch

method

1. Halve the bacon rashers lengthwise and wrap a strip round each chunk of banana.

2. Cut the chicken into bite-sized pieces and thread onto a couple of skewers, alternating with the bacon-wrapped banana.

3. Mix the honey, Worcester sauce and lemon juice together and brush onto the kebabs.

4. Cook the kebabs under a hot grill, turning 3 or 4 times.

5. Combine the satay sauce ingredients and serve with the cooked kebabs on a bed of spiced rice (see page 108), with a salad.

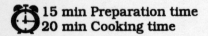 15 min Preparation time
20 min Cooking time

CHICKEN PAPRIKA

ingredients	Metric	Imperial	American
Boned and skinned chicken breast	1	1	1
Olive oil	10 ml	2 tsp	2 tsp
Lemon juice	10 ml	2 tsp	2 tsp
Paprika	2.5 ml	½ tsp	½ tsp
Black pepper			

method

1. Cut the chicken into bite-sized cubes and put them into a small bowl

2. Mix together the olive oil, lemon juice, paprika and a good sprinkling of black pepper. Pour over the chicken and leave to marinate for 10 – 15 minutes.

3. Line the grill pan with foil to catch the juices. Grill the chicken cubes for 10 – 12 minutes, turning them from time to time and basting them with the juices that form in the foil.

4. Spoon the cooked chicken onto a bed of rice and pour the juices left in the foil over the top.

5. Serve with a salad.

5 min Preparation time
(plus 10 min marinating time)
12 min Cooking time

Eggs

If you keep a few eggs in the fridge you need never be at a loss for ideas for a quick meal. Eggs have a very high food value - they contain protein, as well as vitamins A, B, D, and iron and calcium in the yolk. The following dishes are all substantial enough to be a main meal, eaten with some crusty bread and perhaps a small salad.

SPANISH OMELETTE

For this omelette you can use left-over boiled potato from a previous meal, in which case the cooking time will be 10-15 minutes shorter. Cook the onions on their own until soft, then mix with the cooked potato and eggs and continue as below.

ingredients	Metric	Imperial	American
Large potato, peeled	*1*	*1*	*1*
Small onion, peeled	*1*	*1*	*1*
Cooking oil	*15 ml*	*1 tbsp*	*1 tbsp*
Salt			
Eggs	*2*	*2*	*2*

method

1. Cut the potatoes and onion into dice and mix them together.

2. Heat the oil in a frying-pan, add the potato-onion mixture, sprinkle with salt, and fry slowly for 15-20 minutes until soft but not crisp. Remove from the pan with a slotted spoon.

3. Beat the eggs and mix with the cooked potato and onion.

4. Heat a little more oil in the pan until it is smoking hot, then pour in the egg mixture.

5. Cook for 2-3 minutes, until the egg is set but still a little moist.

6. To cook the top of the omelette, slide the frying pan under a hot grill.

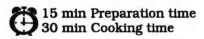 15 min Preparation time
30 min Cooking time

PIPERADE

ingredients	Metric	Imperial	American
Eggs	2	2	2
Salt and pepper			
Cooking oil	15 ml	1 tbsp	1 tbsp
Small onion, peeled and sliced	1	1	1
Green pepper, sliced	½	½	½
Clove of garlic, chopped	1	1	1
Tomato, sliced	1	1	1

method

1. Break the eggs into a mixing bowl, add salt and pepper and beat with a fork.

2. Heat the oil in a frying pan and cook the onion, green pepper and garlic until soft.

3. Add the tomatoes and continue cooking for another 2-3 minutes.

4. Pour the beaten eggs into the frying pan and stir gently with a fish slice. Cook on a low heat until the eggs are set but still moist.

5. To cook the top, slide the frying pan under a hot grill.

10 min Preparation time
15 min Cooking time

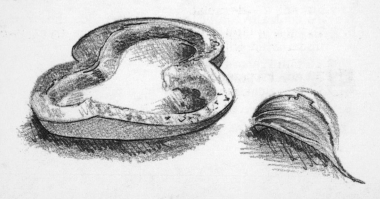

ITALIAN FRITTATA

The classic Italian dish is baked in the oven, but this is a simpler and quicker variation, finished off under the grill.

ingredients	Metric	Imperial	American
Courgette	*1*	*1*	*1*
Salt			
Eggs	*2*	*2*	*2*
Milk	*15 ml*	*1 tbsp*	*1 tbsp*
Black pepper			
Cooking oil	*15 ml*	*1 tbsp*	*1 tbsp*
Small onion, peeled and sliced	*1*	*1*	*1*
Button mushrooms	*50 g*	*2 oz*	*2 oz*

method

1. Chop the courgette into ½ inch/1 cm slices, put into a sieve and sprinkle with a little salt. Leave to drain for 15 minutes, then pat dry with a paper towel.

2. Break the eggs into a basin, add the milk and season with salt and pepper. Beat well with a fork.

3. Heat the oil in a frying pan and gently fry the courgette slices, onion and mushrooms for 5 minutes.

4. Pour the beaten eggs into the pan and stir gently with a fish slice. Cook gently until the egg is set but still a little moist.

5. To cook the top of the frittata, slide the frying pan under a hot grill.

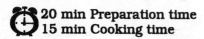 20 min Preparation time
15 min Cooking time

PASTA OMELETTE

ingredients	Metric	Imperial	American
Cold cooked pasta shapes	50 g	2 oz	2 oz
Cooking oil	15 ml	1 tbsp	1 tbsp
Spring onions, chopped	2-3	2-3	2-3
Eggs	2	2	2
Parmesan cheese	15 ml	1 tbsp	1 tbsp
Worcester sauce	2.5 ml	½ tsp	½ tsp

method

1. Heat the oil in a frying pan and gently fry the spring onion for 2 minutes.

2. Stir in the pasta.

3. Beat the eggs with the Parmesan cheese and Worcestershire sauce.

4. Pour over the pasta and cook until the base is set.

5. Put under a hot grill to brown the top.

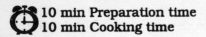 10 min Preparation time
10 min Cooking time

RICE OMELETTE

ingredients	Metric	Imperial	American
Cooked rice	50 g	2 oz	2 oz
Cooking oil	15 ml	1 tbsp	1 tbsp
Small onion, peeled and sliced	1	1	1
Cheddar cheese, grated	25 g	1 oz	1 oz
Chopped parsley	15 ml	1 tbsp	1 tbsp
Eggs	2	2	2
Salt and pepper			

method

1. Heat the oil in a frying pan and gently fry the sliced onion for 2 minutes.

2. Stir in the rice and heat through for another 2 minutes.

3. Stir in the cheese and parsley.

4. Beat the eggs and season with salt and pepper. Pour over the rice in the frying pan and cook until the base is set.

5. Put under a hot grill to brown the top.

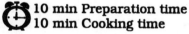 10 min Preparation time
10 min Cooking time

PIZZA OMELETTE

This omelette has a savoury tomato and cheese flavoured topping rather like a pizza.

ingredients	Metric	Imperial	American
Eggs	2	2	2
Salt and pepper			
Cold water	*10 ml*	*2 tsp*	*2 tsp*
Butter	*25 g*	*1 oz*	*1 oz*
Small onion, peeled and sliced	*1*	*1*	*1*
Tomato purée	*5 ml*	*1 tsp*	*1 tsp*
Mixed dried herbs	*pinch*	*pinch*	*pinch*
Bacon rashers	*2*	*2*	*2*
Cheddar cheese, grated	*25 g*	*1 oz*	*1 oz*

method

1. Break the eggs into a mixing bowl. Add a pinch of salt and pepper and the cold water, and mix thoroughly with a fork. Put to one side while you prepare the topping.

2. Melt the butter in a saucepan and cook the onion gently for 4-5 minutes, until soft.

3. Add the tomato purée and mixed herbs and cook for another minute. Remove from the heat and set aside.

4. Using scissors remove the rind from the bacon rashers and cut into small pieces.

5. Heat a frying pan and fry the bacon pieces until the fat runs and bacon is browned. Lift out and keep on one side.

6. Pour the beaten eggs into the still hot frying pan. Stir gently with a fish slice and continue cooking on a low heat until the eggs are set underneath but still moist on top.

7. Take the pan off the heat and cover the omelette with the tomato and onion mixture.

8. Arrange the bacon pieces on top, and sprinkle with grated cheese.

9. Put the omelette under a hot grill just long enough for the cheese to melt and brown.

10. Slide the omelette out of the pan onto a hot plate.

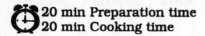 20 min Preparation time
20 min Cooking time

ITALIAN SCRAMBLED EGGS

ingredients	Metric	Imperial	American
Eggs	2	2	2
Milk	30 ml	2 tbsp	2 tbsp
Salt and pepper			
Butter or margarine	25 g	1 oz	1 oz
Green pepper, chopped	½	½	½
Small onion, peeled and chopped	½	½	½
Button mushrooms, sliced	3	3	3
Pepperoni sausage, chopped	25 g	1 oz	1 oz

method

1. Break the eggs into a bowl, add the milk and season with salt and pepper. Beat well with a fork.

2. Melt the butter in a saucepan and gently fry the green pepper, onion and mushrooms for 3 minutes.

3. Add the pepperoni sausage.

4. Pour the beaten eggs into the saucepan and cook gently, stirring all the time, until the egg is thick and creamy.

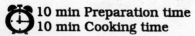 10 min Preparation time
10 min Cooking time

EGG FLORENTINE

ingredients	Metric	Imperial	American
Eggs	*2*	*2*	*2*
Small packet frozen spinach	*1*	*1*	*1*
Cheese sauce (see page 134)			

method

1. Cook the eggs in boiling water for 8 minutes. Plunge into cold water and remove the shells.

2. Meanwhile cook the spinach according to the instructions on the packet.

3. Make the cheese sauce (see page 134).

4. Put the spinach into a heatproof dish and arrange the eggs on top. Pour over the cheese sauce.

5. Brown under a hot grill

6. Serve with toast.

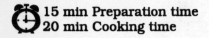 15 min Preparation time
20 min Cooking time

CURRIED EGGS AND RICE

ingredients	Metric	Imperial	American
Eggs	2	2	2
Long grain rice	75-100 g	3-4 oz	3-4 oz
Curry sauce (see page 132)	300 ml	½ pint	1¼ cups

method

1. Cook the eggs in boiling water for 8 minutes. Plunge into cold water and remove the shells.

2. Meanwhile cook the rice (see page 106).

3. Heat the curry sauce in a saucepan, add the hardboiled eggs and simmer gently for 10 minutes.

4. Pile the cooked rice onto a plate and top with the curried eggs.

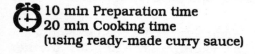
10 min Preparation time
20 min Cooking time
(using ready-made curry sauce)

PROVENÇALE EGGS

ingredients	Metric	Imperial	American
Olive oil	15 ml	1 tbsp	1 tbsp
Small onion, peeled and chopped	1	1	1
Green pepper, chopped	½	½	½
Courgette, sliced	1	1	1
Clove of garlic, crushed	1	1	1
Tomatoes	2	2	2
Salt and pepper			
Eggs	2	2	2
Grated cheese	25 g	1 oz	1 oz

method

1. Heat the oil in a frying pan and fry the onion and pepper until soft.

2. Add the courgette and cook until brown on both sides.

3. Add the garlic, tomatoes, and a good seasoning of salt and pepper. Continue cooking for another minute.

4. Spoon the mixture into a heatproof dish, leaving spaces for the eggs. Break the eggs into the spaces.

5. Sprinkle the grated cheese on top.

6. Put the dish under a preheated grill and cook for about 10 minutes, or until the eggs are set.

7. Eat with French bread.

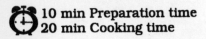
10 min Preparation time
20 min Cooking time

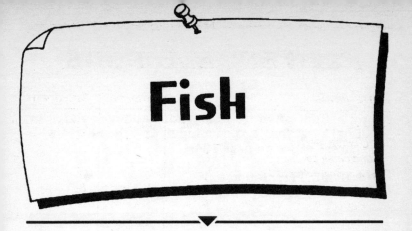

Fish

Fish is extremely nutritious, being high in protein and low in fats. It is also an ideal food for one-person catering. Most supermarkets now have a good fish counter, where you can buy a single fish, or fillet - and it is so quick to cook. There is no need for fish to be boring - just try some of the tasty recipes below.

Fish with Cheese Sauce

Cook a fillet of white fish (cod, haddock, plaice or whiting) by grilling or poaching it, and then serve with the cheese sauce on page 134.

⏰ 10 min Preparation time
10 min Cooking time

To Grill Fish

Heat the grill. Put a knob of butter in a fireproof dish and put it under the grill to melt. Remove the dish and place the fillet in it, skin side down. Spoon a little of the melted butter over the fish, and season with salt and pepper. Put the dish back under the heat for 5-6 minutes, until the fish is cooked (the flesh will flake when you prod it with a fork).

⏰ 2 - 3 min Preparation time
5 - 6 min Cooking time

To Poach Fish

Put ½ cup milk and ½ cup water into a saucepan and bring it to the boil. Add the fillet of fish, reduce the heat and cover with a lid. Simmer for 5-6 minutes, until the fish flakes when you prod it with a fork.

⏰ 2 - 3 min Preparation time
5 - 6 min Cooking time

COD WITH LIME AND CORIANDER

ingredients	Metric	Imperial	American
Cod fillet	175-225 g	6-8 oz	6-8 oz
Flour	25 g	1 oz	1 oz
Salt and black pepper			
Clove of garlic, crushed	1	1	1
Mustard	5 ml	1 tsp	1 tsp
Lime	1	1	1
Olive oil	30 ml	2 tbsp	2 tbsp
Fresh coriander leaves, chopped	15 ml	1 tbsp	1 tbsp

method

1. Remove the skin from the cod fillet and wipe with kitchen paper.

2. Put the flour onto a plate, season with salt and pepper, then coat the fish, pressing well on both sides. Set aside.

3. Mix together the garlic, mustard, juice and rind of the lime, olive oil, and coriander. Season with salt and pepper.

4. Heat a little olive oil in a frying pan. When hot, add the fish fillet and fry for 3 minutes on each side, until crisp and golden.

5. Pour the lime mixture around the fish and continue cooking for another 2-3 minutes.

6. Serve with new boiled potatoes and cooked vegetables.

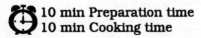 10 min Preparation time
10 min Cooking time

COD WITH GREEN PEPPER

ingredients	Metric	Imperial	American
Cod fillet	175-225 g	6-8 oz	6-8 oz
Oil	15 ml	1 tbsp	1 tbsp
Green pepper, chopped	½	½	½
Tomato sauce	110 ml	4 fl oz	½ cup
Lemon juice	15 ml	1 tbsp	1 tbsp
Worcestershire sauce	5 ml	1 tsp	1 tsp
Salt and pepper			

method

1. Heat the oil in a frying pan and cook the green pepper for 3 minutes.

2. Move it to one side of the pan and add the cod fillet.

3. Cook the fish on both sides until lightly browned.

4. Add the tomato sauce, lemon juice and Worcestershire sauce. Season with salt and pepper.

5. Cover with a lid (use a plate if the frying pan does not have one) and cook over a low heat for 5 minutes, or until the fish flakes easily with a fork.

6. Serve with rice or boiled potatoes, cooked vegetables or a salad.

10 min Preparation time
10 min Cooking time

SESAME PLAICE

ingredients	Metric	Imperial	American
Plaice fillet	175-225 g	6-8 oz	6-8 oz
Butter or margarine	15 g	½ oz	½ oz
Spring onions, chopped	3	3	3
Lemon juice	10 ml	2 tsp	2 tsp
Sesame seeds	5 ml	1 tsp	1 tsp
Salt and pepper			

method

1. Melt the butter in a saucepan.

2. Fold the plaice fillet in half, and put it into the saucepan with the chopped spring onions.

3. Cover and cook gently for 3-4 minutes, turning once.

4. Add the lemon juice and sesame seeds. Season with salt and pepper.

5. Cook for another minute.

6. Serve with rice and a salad.

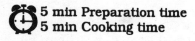
5 min Preparation time
5 min Cooking time

SPICY PLAICE

ingredients	Metric	Imperial	American
Plaice fillet	175-225g	6-8 oz	6-8 oz
Natural yoghurt	15 ml	1 tbsp	1 tbsp
Tandoori or tikka mix	5 ml	1 tsp	1 tsp
Oil	5 ml	1 tsp	1 tsp
Salt	pinch	pinch	pinch

method

1. Mix the yoghurt, spices, oil and salt together.

2. Lay the plaice fillet on the grill pan and brush with the spicy yoghurt mixture.

3. Cook under a medium grill for 4-5 minutes.

4. Serve with rice and a salad.

5 min Preparation time
5 min Cooking time

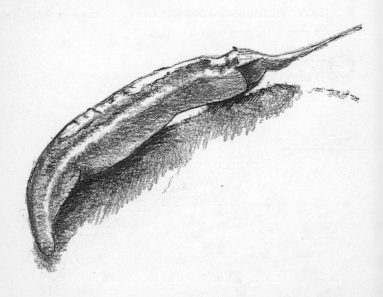

GRILLED HERRING, MACKEREL OR TROUT

Most of the fish you buy these days is ready prepared. If not, ask the fishmonger to prepare it for you.

ingredients	Metric	Imperial	American
Ready prepared herring (mackerel or trout)	*175-225 g*	*6-8 oz*	*6-8 oz*
Oil or melted butter			

method

1. Rinse the fish under cold running water and pat dry with kitchen paper.

2. Brush with oil or melted butter.

3. Lay the fish on the grill rack and cook under a medium grill for 7 minutes.

4. Turn the fish over and grill the other side.

5. Serve with new boiled potatoes, cooked vegetables or a salad.

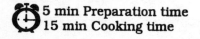 5 min Preparation time
15 min Cooking time

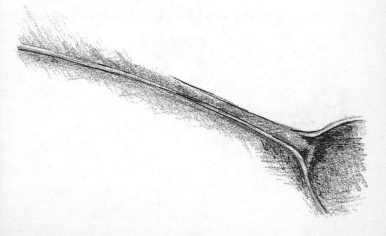

MUSTARD HERRING

A mackerel fillet tastes just as good as herring.

ingredients	Metric	Imperial	American
Herring fillet	*175-225 g*	*6-8 oz*	*6-8 oz*
Mustard	*5 ml*	*1 tsp*	*1 tsp*
Lemon juice	*5 ml*	*1 tsp*	*1 tsp*
Salt and pepper			

method

1. Lay the herring fillet on the grill pan skin side down.

2. Spread with mustard. Sprinkle with lemon juice, salt and pepper.

3. Grill for 6-8 minutes.

4. Serve with potatoes and cooked vegetables.

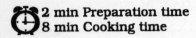
2 min Preparation time
8 min Cooking time

KEDGEREE

ingredients	Metric	Imperial	American
Smoked haddock	50-75 g	2-3 oz	2-3 oz
Butter	15 g	½ oz	½ oz
Cooked rice	1 cup	1 cup	1 cup
Hardboiled egg, chopped	1	1	1
Salt and pepper			

method

1. Put the smoked haddock into a saucepan with a little water and cook for about 5 minutes, until the fish flakes. Remove the skin.

2. Rinse out the saucepan, add the butter, and when it has melted stir in the flaked fish, cooked rice and egg.

3. Season with salt and pepper, and cook over a gentle heat for 8-10 minutes.

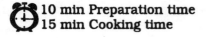 10 min Preparation time
15 min Cooking time

SMOKED HADDOCK WITH PASTA

ingredients	Metric	Imperial	American
Smoked haddock	50-75 g	2-3 oz	2-3 oz
Milk	150 ml	¼ pint	½ cup
Pasta shapes	50-75 g	2-3 oz	2-3 oz
Margarine	15 g	½ oz	½ oz
Flour	15 g	½ oz	½ oz
Hardboiled egg, chopped	1	1	1
Tomato, chopped	1	1	1
Salt and pepper			
Cheddar cheese, grated	25 g	1 oz	1 oz

method

1. Cook the fish in the milk for about 5 minutes. Pour off the milk into a jug. Remove the skin of the fish and flake the flesh. Put milk and fish aside.

2. Cook the pasta according to the instructions on the packet.

3. Melt the margarine in a saucepan, stir in the flour and cook for 1 minute.

4. Remove the saucepan from the heat and stir in the reserved milk.

5. Return the saucepan to the heat and bring to the boil, stirring all the time to stop lumps forming. Turn down the heat. Simmer for 2 minutes.

6. Add the flaked fish, egg, tomato, salt, pepper, and drained pasta. Mix well together and spoon into a heatproof dish.

7. Sprinkle grated cheese on top and put under a hot grill until golden brown.

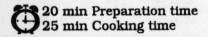
20 min Preparation time
25 min Cooking time

FISH KEBABS

ingredients	Metric	Imperial	American
Fillet of cod	150 g	6 oz	6 oz
Green pepper	½	½	½
Button mushrooms	6-8	6-8	6-8
Oil or butter			
Salt and pepper			
Lemon juice			

method

1. Cut the fish and green pepper into neat pieces. Push onto two skewers, alternating fish, pepper and mushrooms.

2. Brush with oil or melted butter, and season lightly with salt and pepper. Sprinkle with lemon juice.

3. Cook under a hot grill for 8-10 minutes, turning several times.

4. Serve the kebabs on a bed of rice, with rings of lemon or tomato sauce (see page 133).

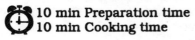
10 min Preparation time
10 min Cooking time

FRIED PLAICE OR LEMON SOLE FILLET

ingredients	Metric	Imperial	American
Plaice or lemon sole fillet	1	1	1
Milk	15 ml	1 tbsp	1 tbsp
Flour			
Salt and pepper			
Butter			
Cooking oil	15 ml	1 tbsp	1 tbsp
Lemon juice			

method

1. Spoon the milk into a small bowl. Dip both sides of the fish fillet into the milk.

2. Sprinkle a little flour into another bowl and season with salt and pepper. Dip the fish into the flour so that it is coated on both sides.

3. Put a knob of butter and the oil into a frying pan. Heat until the butter has melted and then put the fish fillet into the pan skin side up. Cook for 3-4 minutes, then turn over and cook the other side.

4. When both sides are golden brown lift the fillet onto a warmed plate with a fish slice.

5. Sprinkle a little lemon juice over the fish, and serve with new boiled potatoes and fresh vegetables.

10 min Preparation time
10 min Cooking time

ITALIAN STYLE WHITING

ingredients	Metric	Imperial	American
Whiting fillet	*1*	*1*	*1*
Lemon juice	*5 ml*	*1 tsp*	*1 tsp*
Pasta shells	*75 g*	*3 oz*	*3 oz*
Tomato sauce (see page 133)			

method

1. Put the whiting fillet into a saucepan with a little water and the lemon juice. Bring to the boil and then reduce the heat and cover with a lid. Simmer for 5-6 minutes, until the fish flakes when you prod it with a fork.

2. Meanwhile cook the pasta according to the instructions on the packet.

3. Make the tomato sauce (see page 133).

4. Serve the whiting with pasta, tomato sauce and a green salad.

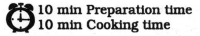 10 min Preparation time
10 min Cooking time

HAM

In this section you will find some ideas for using cooked ham that are more interesting than simply putting it in a sandwich. Uncooked ham (gammon steaks) comes under the Meat section. See also ham risotto (page 110), ham fried rice (page 111), pasta shells with ham and cream sauce (page 77), croque monsieur (page 16).

HAM AND POTATO CAKES

ingredients	Metric	Imperial	American
Cooked ham	50 g	2 oz	2 oz
Small onion	1	1	1
Large potato	1	1	1
Self-raising flour	25 g	1 oz	1 oz
Egg, beaten	1	1	1
Milk	15 ml	1 tbsp	1 tbsp
Salt and pepper			
Cooking oil	30 ml	2 tbsp	2 tbsp

method

1   Chop the ham. Peel and grate the onion and potato.

2   Mix together the ham, onion, potato and flour. Beat in the egg and milk. Season with salt and pepper.

3.   Heat the oil in a frying pan. When it is really hot drop in spoonfuls of the potato mixture. Fry for 2 minutes, then turn and fry on the other side.

4.   Lower the heat and cook for a further 5-6 minutes.

5.   Drain on kitchen paper.

6.   Serve with green beans, peas or sweetcorn.

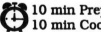 10 min Preparation time
10 min Cooking time

STUFFED HAM ROLLS

ingredients	Metric	Imperial	American
Slices of ham	2	2	2
Cooked potatoes	2-3	2-3	2-3
Sticks of celery	1	1	1
Gherkins	4	4	4
Mayonnaise	15 ml	1 tbsp	1 tbsp
Mustard	2.5 ml	½ tsp	½ tsp

method

1. Dice the cooked potatoes and celery. Chop the gherkins.

2. Stir the mustard into the mayonnaise.

3. Mix all the ingredients together and spoon onto the slices of ham.

4. Roll up the ham and serve with salad and crusty bread.

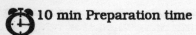 10 min Preparation time

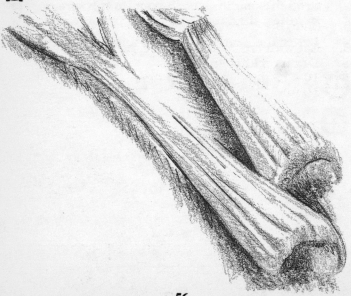

HAM OMELETTE

ingredients	Metric	Imperial	American
Eggs	2	2	2
Salt and pepper			
Oil	10 ml	2 tsp	2 tsp
Slice of ham, chopped	1	1	1

method

1. Break the eggs into a basin. Add salt and pepper and a tablespoon of cold water. Beat together with a fork.

2. Heat a frying pan to a fairly high temperature and add the oil.

3. Pour in the eggs, swirling them over the bottom of the pan. As the egg sets, draw the cooked bits to the centre with a fish slice or spatula, allowing the uncooked egg to run to the sides. Tilt the pan as you work.

4. Before the omelette is completely set, sprinkle the chopped ham onto one half, and fold the other half over.

5. Slide the omelette out onto a warm plate.

6. Eat with crusty bread and a green salad.

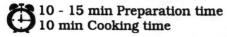 10 - 15 min Preparation time
10 min Cooking time

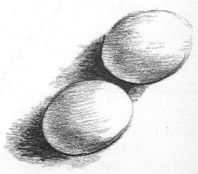

HASH

This is a good way of using up some leftover cooked potatoes. You can substitute corned beef for the ham.

ingredients	Metric	Imperial	American
Cooking oil	*15 ml*	*1 tbsp*	*1 tbsp*
Small onion, peeled and chopped	*1*	*1*	*1*
Cooked ham or corned beef	*50 g*	*2 oz*	*2 oz*
Cooked potatoes, mashed with a little milk	*2-3*	*2-3*	*2-3*
Salt and pepper			

method

1. Heat the oil in a frying pan and gently cook the onion for about 5 minutes, or until soft.

2. Mix the ham with the mashed potato and season with salt and pepper.

3. Spoon the mixture into the frying pan, pressing it well down to cover the base.

4. Cook over a medium heat until the underside is golden brown, then turn the hash over with a fish slice and cook the other side.

5. Serve with some grilled tomato and/or peas.

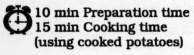 10 min Preparation time
15 min Cooking time
(using cooked potatoes)

HAM AND CHEESE PIZZA

This quick and easy pizza is cooked in a frying pan

ingredients	Metric	Imperial	American
Self-raising flour	100 g	4 oz	4 oz
Salt and pepper			
Vegetable or sunflower oil	30 ml	2 tbsp	2 tbsp
water	30 ml	2 tbsp	2 tbsp
Tomatoe purée	30 ml	2 tbsp	2 tbsp
Tin chopped tomatoes	200 g	7 oz	7 oz
Cooked ham, cut into strips	50 g	2 oz	2 oz
Cheddar cheese, grated	50 g	2 oz	2 oz
Dried mixed herbs	5 ml	1 tsp	1 tsp

method

1. Put the flour into a mixing bowl. Add a little salt and pepper. Make a well in the centre of the flour and pour in 1 tablespoon oil and water. Mix to a soft dough.

2. On a floured surface, roll out the dough to a circle that will fit your frying pan.

3. Heat a little oil in the frying pan. Fry the dough for about 5 minutes, until the base is cooked and lightly brown. Turn out onto a plate.

4. Add the remaining oil to the frying pan and slide the dough back in, cooked side upwards.

5. Spread over the tomato purée, then top with the tomatoes, ham and grated cheese. Sprinkle with dried herbs.

6. Cook until the underside is browned, and then slide the frying pan under a hot grill until the cheese on top is bubbling.

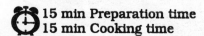
15 min Preparation time
15 min Cooking time

MEAT

Putting a pork chop under the grill is not the only answer for solo meat-eaters. Try some of the following quick and easy ways of making a more interesting meal. You will find other ideas in Stir-fry (page 144) and Three Meals in One (page 156).

MINUTE STEAK

ingredients	Metric	Imperial	American
Minute steak	1	1	1
Garlic salt			
Black pepper			
Oil	15 ml	1 tbsp	1 tbsp
Butter	12.5 g	½ oz	½ oz
Spring onions, chopped	2	2	2
Lemon juice	5 ml	1 tsp	1 tsp
Worcester sauce	5 ml	1 tsp	1 tsp
Mustard	¼ tsp	¼ tsp	¼ tsp

method

1. Sprinkle garlic salt and black pepper on both sides of the steak.

2. Heat the oil in a frying pan and fry the steak for 2 minutes on each side, on a medium heat.

3. Remove the steak from the frying pan and put it on a warmed plate.

4. Drain the oil from the pan, melt the butter, and add the chopped spring onions. Fry gently for 2 minutes.

5. Add the lemon juice, Worcester sauce and mustard.

6. Heat through gently, then pour the sauce over the steak.

7. Serve with new boiled potatoes and peas, or a salad.

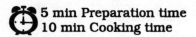
5 min Preparation time
10 min Cooking time

MEATBALLS

These quantities are enough for two meals. For variety, serve one portion with mashed potato and cooked vegetables, and the remainder with spaghetti and a green salad. Keep the leftover portion in the refrigerator overnight and make sure it is thoroughly reheated the following day. Meatballs freeze well to eat at a later date.

ingredients	Metric	Imperial	American
Minced beef	*350 g*	*12 oz*	*12 oz*
Onion, peeled and finely chopped	*1*	*1*	*1*
Salt and pepper			
Slice of white bread	*1*	*1*	*1*
Milk	*15 ml*	*1 tbsp*	*1 tbsp*
Small egg, beaten	*1*	*1*	*1*
Flour	*25 g*	*1 oz*	*1 oz*
Butter	*25 g*	*1 oz*	*1 oz*
Beef stock (made with a stock cube)	*300 ml*	*½ pint*	*1¼ cups*
Tomato purée	*10 ml*	*2 tsp*	*2 tsp*
Cornflour	*5 ml*	*1 tsp*	*1 tsp*
Vinegar	*5 ml*	*1 tsp*	*1 tsp*

method

1. Put the minced beef and onion into a mixing bowl and season well with salt and pepper.

2. Put the slice of bread into a small basin and add the milk. Leave to soak for a couple of minutes, then squeeze out any excess moisture.

3. Add the bread to the meat mixture.

4. Stir in enough beaten egg to make a soft, but not runny, mixture that you can shape into 8 balls.

5. Sprinkle the flour onto a plate and season with salt and pepper. Roll the meatballs in the seasoned flour.

6. Melt the butter in a frying pan and fry the meatballs until they are golden brown all over - shake the pan gently as you cook and they will keep their shape.

7. Add the stock and tomato purée and stir to mix well.

8. Bring to the boil and simmer for 30 minutes.

9. Blend the cornflour with a little water and add to the sauce to thicken it.

10. Before serving check the seasoning and add the vinegar to sharpen the flavour of the sauce.

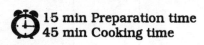 15 min Preparation time
45 min Cooking time

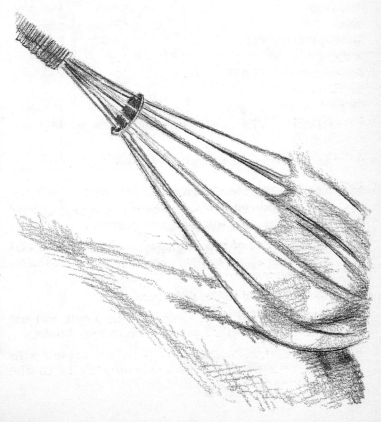

BOLOGNESE SAUCE FOR PASTA

This meat sauce can be served with any type of pasta. The quantities given will make enough for two meals. Freeze the second portion in a small container to eat at a later date.

ingredients	Metric	Imperial	American
Oil	*15 ml*	*1 tbsp*	*1 tbsp*
Onion, peeled and chopped	*1*	*1*	*1*
Clove of garlic, crushed	*1*	*1*	*1*
Minced beef	*250 g*	*8 oz*	*8 oz*
Tin chopped tomatoes	*200 g*	*7 oz*	*7 oz*
Tomato purée (paste)	*15 ml*	*1 tbsp*	*1 tbsp*
Dried mixed herbs	*5 ml*	*1 tsp*	*1 tsp*
Freshly-ground black pepper			

method

1. Heat the oil and fry the onions and garlic until soft.

2. Add the minced beef and fry until brown.

3. Add the tomatoes, tomato purée, herbs, salt and pepper and cook for 30 minutes.

4. Meanwhile cook the pasta.

5. To serve, spoon the Bolognese sauce over cooked pasta and sprinkle with parmesan cheese.

15 min Preparation time
40 min Cooking time

CHILLI CON CARNE

These quantities are enough for two meals, served with rice, pitta bread or a jacket potato. If you plan to eat the second portion the following day, keep it in the refrigerator overnight and reheat thoroughly. Otherwise you could freeze the second portion in a small container to eat at a later date.

ingredients	Metric	Imperial	American
Cooking oil	15 ml	1 tbsp	1 tbsp
Onion, peeled and sliced	1	1	1
Clove of garlic, crushed	1	1	1
Green pepper, sliced	½	½	½
Minced beef	225 g	8 oz	8 oz
Tin tomatoes	200 g	7 oz	7 oz
Chilli powder	5 ml	1 tsp	1 tsp
(more if you like it hot!)			
Salt and pepper			
Tin red kidney beans	200 g	7 oz	7 oz

method

1. Heat the oil in a saucepan and cook the onion, garlic and pepper gently for 5 minutes.

2. Add the meat and fry until browned.

3. Add the tomatoes and chilli powder. Season with salt and pepper.

4. Bring to the boil and simmer for 30 minutes.

5. Drain the red kidney beans through a sieve, rinse well and add to the saucepan.

6. Cook for a further 30 minutes.

7. Serve with rice.

10 min Preparation time
1 hour Cooking time

PORK PAPRIKA

ingredients	Metric	Imperial	American
Lean pork, cubed	150 g	6 oz	6 oz
Oil	10 ml	2 tsp	2 tsp
Small onion, peeled and finely chopped	1	1	1
Clove of garlic, crushed	1	1	1
Paprika	5 ml	1 tsp	1 tsp
Cayenne	pinch	pinch	pinch
Salt			
Tin tomatoes	200 g	7 oz	7 oz
Natural yoghurt	15 ml	1 tbsp	1 tbsp

method

1. Heat the oil in a saucepan until it is very hot and quicky fry the cubed pork until it is browned. Remove from the saucepan and keep aside.

2. In the same oil, fry the onion and garlic until soft.

3. Stir in the paprika, cayenne and a little salt.

4. Add the meat and tomatoes, bring to the boil, cover and simmer for 40 minutes - or until the pork is tender.

5. Add the yoghurt just before serving.

6. Serve with rice or noodles and a green salad.

10 min Preparation time
45 min Cooking time

PORK IN WINE SAUCE

ingredients	Metric	Imperial	American
Pork chop or steak	1	1	1
Salt and pepper			
Flour	25 g	1 oz	1 oz
Butter	12.5 g	½ oz	½ oz
Small onion, peeled and finely chopped	1	1	1
Tomato purée	2.5 ml	½ tsp	½ tsp
White wine	30 ml	2 tbsp	2 tbsp

method

1. Put the flour, seasoned with salt and pepper, onto a plate and coat the chop on both sides. Shake off any surplus flour.

2. Melt the butter in a saucepan and fry the chop gently on both sides, until golden brown.

3. Remove the chop from the pan and add the onion. Cook gently until soft.

4. Stir in the tomato purée and wine. Cover with a lid and simmer for 15-20 minutes, or until the pork is tender.

5. Serve with boiled potatoes and vegetables.

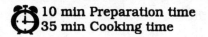 10 min Preparation time
35 min Cooking time

PORK WITH CRUNCHY RED CABBAGE

Choose a thin, lean boneless chop for this dish.

ingredients	Metric	Imperial	American
Pork chop	1	1	1
Wine vinegar	15 ml	1 tbsp	1 tbsp
Chopped fresh herbs	15 ml	1 tbsp	1 tbsp
(or 1 tsp dried mixed herbs)			
Honey	5 ml	1 tsp	1 tsp
Lemon juice	10 ml	2 tsp	2 tsp
Salt and pepper			
Cooking oil	10 ml	2 tsp	2 tsp
Small onion, peeled and			
chopped	1	1	1
Red cabbage, shredded	50 g	2 oz	2 oz
Small red apple, chopped	1	1	1

method

1. Slash the pork chop with a knife in a crisscross pattern.

2. Mix together the vinegar, herbs, honey, lemon juice and seasoning. Spoon over the pork chop and leave to marinate for half an hour.

3. Lift the chop from the marinade and cook under a hot grill for 4-5 minutes on each side.

4. Meanwhile heat the oil in a frying pan and cook the onion for 2 minutes.

5. Add the shredded cabbage, chopped apple, and the remaining marinade mixture. Stir-fry for 4-5 minutes, until the liquid has evaporated.

6. Serve the cooked pork chop with the red cabbage and mashed potato or rice.

10 min Preparation time (plus marinating time)
20 min Cooking time

SHISH KEBABS

ingredients	Metric	Imperial	American
Boned lamb	150 g	6 oz	6 oz
Oil	15 ml	1 tbsp	1 tbsp
Vinegar	15 ml	1 tbsp	1 tbsp
Salt and pepper			
Small onion, peeled and cut into cubes	1	1	1
Tin pineapple cubes	200 g	7 oz	7 oz
Green pepper, cut into cubes	½	½	½

method

1. Cut the meat into cubes and put into a small basin. Add the oil, vinegar, salt and pepper. Stir so that all the meat is covered, and put aside to marinate for a couple of hours.

2. When you are ready to cook, remove the meat from the marinade with a fish slice. Thread the meat onto skewers, alternating with the onion, pineapple and green pepper.

3. Cook under a hot grill, turning frequently, until the meat is browned on all sides.

4. Serve with spiced rice and a salad.

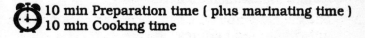 10 min Preparation time (plus marinating time)
10 min Cooking time

VEAL STEW

ingredients	Metric	Imperial	American
Stewing veal, cubed	150 g	6 oz	6 oz
Butter	12.5 g	½ oz	½ oz
Small onion, peeled and sliced	1	1	1
Flour	12.5 g	½ oz	½ oz
Salt and pepper			
Milk	150 ml	¼ pint	½ cup
Bacon rashers	2	2	2

method

1. Melt the butter in a saucepan and fry the veal and onion for 3-4 minutes.

2. Stir in the flour, salt and pepper and cook for another minute.

3. Add the milk, bring to the boil, then reduce the heat to simmering point. Cover and cook gently for 30 minutes, or until the veal is tender.

4. Meanwhile cut the rashers of bacon in half lengthways, roll up and grill until crisp.

5. Serve the veal stew on a bed of rice, with the bacon rolls arranged on top.

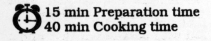 15 min Preparation time
40 min Cooking time

LIVER AND BACON

ingredients	Metric	Imperial	American
Calf's or lamb's liver	100-150 g	4-6 oz	4-6 oz
Salt and pepper			
Butter	12.5 g	½ oz	½ oz
Cooking oil	15 ml	1 tbsp	1 tbsp
Small onion, peeled and sliced	1	1	1
Bacon rasher, chopped	1	1	1
Sherry	30 ml	2 tbsp	2 tbsp
Chopped parsley (optional)	15 ml	1 tbsp	1 tbsp

method

1. Cut the liver into thin slices and season generously with salt and pepper.

2. Heat the butter and oil in a frying pan. Cook the onion on a medium heat until soft. Remove from the pan with a slotted spoon and set aside.

3. Cook the bacon in the frying pan until lightly browned. Remove and set aside.

4. Turn the heat up to high and sauté the slices of liver for 1 minute on each side.

5. Put the onion and bacon back into the pan. Add the sherry and heat until the sauce is bubbling.

6. Stir in the parsley. Eat with potatoes or rice, and a cooked vegetable.

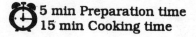 5 min Preparation time
15 min Cooking time

LAMB CHOPS WITH TOMATO SAUCE

ingredients	Metric	Imperial	American
Lamb chops or cutlets	2	2	2
Salt and pepper			
Flour	25 g	1 oz	1 oz
Butter	12.5 g	½ oz	½ oz
Small onion, peeled and finely chopped	1	1	1
Tin condensed tomato soup	½	½	½
Dried herbs	5 ml	1 tsp	1 tsp

method

1. Put the flour, seasoned with salt and pepper, onto a plate and coat the chops on both sides. Shake off any surplus flour.

2. Melt the butter in a saucepan and fry the onion gently for 2-3 minutes.

3. Push the onion to one side of the pan and fry the chops on the other side.

4. Pour over the condensed soup, and sprinkle with herbs.

5. Cover with a lid or plate and simmer for 25-30 minutes, until the chops are tender.

6. Serve with boiled potatoes and vegetables.

10 min Preparation time
35 min Cooking time

GLAZED GAMMON STEAK

ingredients	Metric	Imperial	American
Gammon steak	150 g	6 oz	6 oz
Butter	12.5 g	½ oz	½ oz
Honey	15 ml	1 tbsp	1 tbsp
Mustard	10 ml	2 tsp	2 tsp
Salt and pepper			

method

1. Put the butter into a heatproof dish. Place under a hot grill to allow the butter to melt.

2. Meanwhile mix the honey, mustard, salt and pepper together. Coat the gammon steak on both sides with this mixture.

3. Lay the gammon steak in the dish in which you have melted the butter, and grill for 5 minutes on each side.

4. Serve with spiced rice (see page 108) and a green salad.

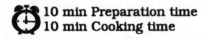 10 min Preparation time
10 min Cooking time

PASTA

Pasta is a nutritious and healthy food that is endlessly versatile if you are cooking for one. It may be bought fresh, which is quicker to cook and tastes better, or in the dried form. The following are the more common types of pasta that you will find in your supermarket.

Spaghetti - long, round, string-like pasta. Comes in various lengths and thicknesses. Vermicelli is thinner; capellini the thinnest.

Tagliatelli - flat, ribbon noodles, made from egg pasta. Comes in strands or nests. There is also a green version.

Macaroni - slightly curved tube pasta of varying size and length.

Rigatoni - fat tube pasta with ridges.

Cannelloni - large, short tubes for stuffing.

Ravioli - squares with serrated edges, traditionally filled with spinach and ricotta cheese, but often with meat.

Lasagne - broad sheets of pasta for baking.

Shapes - shells (conchiglie), bows (farfelle), twists (fusilli), and tubes (penne) come in various sizes, smooth or ridged.

COOKING PASTA

The method is the same for fresh or dried pasta, but the time required will be different - fresh pasta takes about 3 minutes, dried about 12 minutes.

Bring to the boil a large saucepan of water. Add a pinch of salt and a few drops of cooking oil, which will help stop the water boiling over. Put in the pasta - long spaghetti or tagliatelli should be stood up in the saucepan and then pushed down gradually as it softens. Let the water come to the boil again, then lower the heat a little and leave to simmer without a lid until the pasta is just cooked. The pasta should have a slight bite to it, which the Italians call *al dente*.

WAYS TO SERVE BOILED PASTA

Plain
Pasta tastes delicious just on its own. Stir a tablespoon of olive oil into the hot, cooked pasta and sprinkle on plenty of freshly-ground black pepper.

Parmesan cheese
Sprinkle over the hot cooked pasta. Freshy-grated cheese tastes much better than the kind you buy in a drum. However, the latter is more convenient and keeps for a long time in the fridge.

Oil and garlic
Cook 6-8 cloves of chopped garlic in plenty of olive oil and pour it over a dish of hot, cooked pasta. Add 3-4 chopped anchovies, some chopped parsley and a good sprinkling of freshly-ground black pepper. For garlic-lovers only!

Ready-made sauces
Most supermarkets now stock a wide range of sauces in tins and jars to pour over your pasta.

Pesto

Pesto is a strong tangy sauce made from basil and pine nuts. Stir into the cooked pasta, and if you like it, sprinkle Parmesan cheese on top.

Bolognese sauce
See page 162.

Peperonata
See page 184.

FILLINGS FOR RAVIOLI AND CANNELLONI

Meat
Mix together 225 g/8 oz finely-chopped cooked meat, a beaten egg, some chopped parsley, salt, pepper and nutmeg.

Cheese
Mix together 225 g/8 oz ricotta cheese, 30 ml/2 tbsp Parmesan, a beaten egg and some chopped parsley.

Spinach and ricotta
Mix together 100 g/4 oz cooked spinach, 225 g/8 oz ricotta, salt and pepper.

Pasta Shells with Ham and Cream Sauce

ingredients	Metric	Imperial	American
Pasta shells	75-100 g	3-4 oz	3-4 oz
Olive oil	10 ml	2 tsp	2 tsp
Spring onions, sliced	2	2	2
Clove of garlic, crushed	1	1	1
Egg	1	1	1
Cream	30 ml	2 tbsp	2 tbsp
Parmesan cheese	15 ml	1 tbsp	1 tbsp
Salt and pepper			
Cooked ham, cut into strips	50 g	2 oz	2 oz

method

1. Cook the pasta in a large pan of salted water.

2. Meanwhile heat the oil in a small saucepan and fry the onions and garlic for 3-4 minutes, until softened.

3. In a small bowl, beat together the egg, cream, and parmesan. Season with salt and pepper.

4. Drain the pasta into a sieve, and then return it to the pan - but do not put on the heat.

5. Immediately add the beaten egg mixture, cooked onion and garlic, and ham. Toss thoroughly.

6. Serve with a green salad.

15 min Preparation time
20 min Cooking time

PASTA QUILLS IN TOMATO AND BACON SAUCE

ingredients	Metric	Imperial	American
Pasta quills	75-100 g	3-4 oz	3-4 oz
Olive oil	10 ml	2 tsp	2 tsp
Small onion, peeled and sliced	1	1	1
Chilli powder	pinch	pinch	pinch
Bacon, chopped	25-50 g	1-2 oz	1-2 oz
Tomato purée	5 ml	1 tsp	1 tsp
Tin tomatoes	200 g	7 oz	7 oz
Dried basil	2.5 ml	½ tsp	½ tsp
Salt and pepper			
Parmesan			

method

1. Heat the oil in a saucepan and fry the onion gently for 4-5 minutes, until soft.

2. Add the chilli powder and chopped bacon, then cook for another 3-4 minutes.

3. Add the tomato purée, tomatoes, and basil. Season with salt and pepper. Bring to the boil and simmer for 10-15 minutes.

4. Meanwhile, cook the pasta in a large pan of salted water.

5. Drain the pasta well and add it to the hot sauce. Toss thoroughly.

6. Sprinkle with parmesan cheese before eating.

7. Serve with a green salad.

15 min Preparation time
25 min Cooking time

TUNA PASTA

ingredients	Metric	Imperial	American
Pasta shapes	75-100 g	3-4 oz	3-4 oz
Tin tuna in brine	100 g	3½ oz	3½ oz
Tin chopped tomatoes	200 g	7 oz	7 oz
Dried herbs	pinch	pinch	pinch
Black pepper			

method

1. Cook the pasta in salted water, then drain into a sieve.

2. Rinse out the saucepan and dry it.

3. Drain the tuna and put it into the saucepan with the tomatoes and herbs. Heat gently for 5 minutes.

4. Add the drained, cooked pasta and mix everything together thoroughly.

5. Sprinkle with plenty of black pepper.

6. Serve with a green salad.

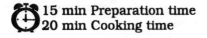 15 min Preparation time
20 min Cooking time

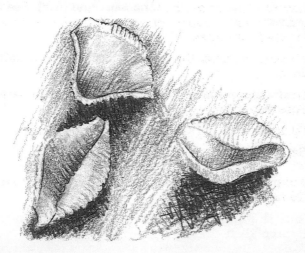

RIGATONI WITH PEPPERONI SAUSAGE

For a real Italian flavour, use Gruyère and mozzarella cheese - but if you don't have them Cheddar will do almost as well.

ingredients	Metric	Imperial	American
Rigatoni	75 g	3 oz	3 oz
Salt and pepper			
Butter or margarine	25 g	1 oz	1 oz
Small smoked sausage	1	1	1
(or a piece of a large one)			
Flour	12.5 g	½ oz	½ oz
Milk	110 ml	4 fl oz	½ cup
Gruyère cheese, grated	25 g	1 oz	1 oz
Tomato purée	15 ml	1 tbsp	1 tbsp
Slices of pepperoni sausage	4	4	4
Slices of mozzarella cheese	2	2	2

method

1. Cook the pasta in a pan of salted water and drain through a sieve.

2. Put the pasta back into the saucepan and season well with salt and pepper.

3. Add half the butter and the smoked sausage cut in to thin slices. Mix well and spoon into a fireproof dish.

4. Rinse out and dry the saucepan, and put it on a low heat. Melt the remaining butter and stir in the flour.

5. Gradually stir in the milk and bring the sauce to the boil so that it thickens.

6. Remove from the heat and stir in the grated cheese.

7. Pour the cheese sauce over the rigatoni in the fireproof dish.

8. Mix the tomato purée with a tablespoon of hot water and pour over the top.

9. Arrange the slices of pepperoni and mozarella on top and put under a hot grill until the cheese is bubbling and golden brown.

10. Serve with a green salad.

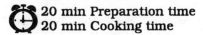
20 min Preparation time
20 min Cooking time

MEAT AND MACARONI

ingredients	Metric	Imperial	American
Cooking oil	15 ml	1 tbsp	1 tbsp
Minced beef	100 g	4 oz	4 oz
Small onion, peeled and sliced	1	1	1
Small green pepper, chopped	1	1	1
Macaroni	75 g	3 oz	3 oz
Tomato juice	1 cup	1 cup	1 cup
Clove of garlic, crushed	1	1	1
Salt and pepper			

method

1. Heat the oil in a saucepan, add the meat, onion and pepper and fry for about 5 minutes, until the meat is browned.

2. Add the macaroni, tomato juice and garlic.

3. Season with salt and pepper.

4. Cover with a lid and simmer for about 20 minutes, until the macaroni is soft.

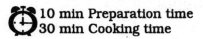
10 min Preparation time
30 min Cooking time

MACARONI, CHEESE AND BACON

ingredients	Metric	Imperial	American
Macaroni	75 g	3 oz	3 oz
Bacon rashers	2	2	2
Small onion, peeled and sliced	1	1	1
Cheddar cheese, grated	25 g	1 oz	1 oz
About ¼ tin of tomato soup, plus the same amount of milk			

method

1. Cook the macaroni in salted water for 10 minutes. Drain into a sieve, rinse under the tap, and set aside.

2. Rinse out and dry the saucepan, then fry the bacon until crisp. Lift out onto a plate and crumble into small pieces.

3. Gently fry the onion in the remaining bacon fat for 2-3 minutes.

4. Add the cooked macaroni, crumbled bacon, cheese soup and milk. Mix thoroughly together and heat gently for a further 2-3 minutes.

5. Turn the mixture into a fireproof dish and put under a hot grill until the top is browned and bubbling.

20 min Preparation time
30 min Cooking time

TAGLIATELLI WITH BACON AND MUSHROOMS

ingredients	Metric	Imperial	American
Tagliatelli	75 g	3 oz	3 oz
Cooking oil	15 ml	1 tbsp	1 tbsp
Mushrooms	50 g	2 oz	2 oz
Clove of garlic, crushed	1	1	1
Smoked bacon rashers, chopped	2	2	2
White wine	15 ml	1 tbsp	1 tbsp
Dried oregano	1.5 ml	1/4 tsp	1/4 tsp
Small knob of butter			
Pepper			

method

1. Cook the tagliatelli according to the instructions on the packet. Drain and set aside.

2. Meanwhile heat the oil in a saucepan and gently fry the mushrooms, garlic and bacon for 5 minutes.

3. Add the wine and continue cooking for another 5 minutes.

4. Stir in the cooked tagliatelli, oregano and butter.

5. Season well with black pepper.

6. Serve with a green salad.

15 min Preparation time
15 min Cooking time

TAGLIATELLI WITH BACON AND PESTO

ingredients	Metric	Imperial	American
Tagliatelli	75 g	3 oz	3 oz
Olive oil	15 ml	1 tbsp	1 tbsp
Unsmoked bacon rashers, chopped	2	2	2
Clove of garlic, crushed	1	1	1
Pesto sauce	15 ml	1 tbsp	1 tbsp
Natural yoghurt or cream	30 ml	2 tbsp	2 tbsp
Parmesan cheese	15 ml	1 tbsp	1 tbsp
Black pepper			
Olives (optional)	6	6	6

method

1. Cook the tagliatelli according to the instructions on the packet. Drain.

2. Meanwhile heat the oil in a frying pan and fry the bacon and garlic for 5 minutes.

3. Add the drained tagliatelli, pesto, yoghurt, and parmesan. Season with black pepper.

4. Spoon onto a warmed plate and arrange olives on top.

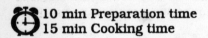
10 min Preparation time
15 min Cooking time

TORTELLINI

Tortellini is little parcels of stuffed pasta. You can buy it fresh or dried, filled with spinach and ricotta or beef and mortadella. A packet of dried tortellini is a very useful item for the store cupboard, as it provides a quick and filling meal. Traditionally, tortellini is added to soups (see page 143). It is equally delicious as a main meal, served with tomato sauce (see page 133) or simply tossed in a little olive oil and sprinkled with grated Parmesan cheese.

TORTELLINI WITH MUSHROOM SAUCE

ingredients	Metric	Imperial	American
Tortellini	75 g	3 oz	3 oz
Butter	12.5 g	½ oz	½ oz
Spring onions, chopped	2	2	2
Clove of garlic, crushed	1	1	1
Mushrooms, sliced	25 g	1 oz	1 oz
Crême fraiche	100 g	4 oz	4 oz
Fresh herbs (parsley, basil, oregano), chopped	15 ml	1 tbsp	1 tbsp
Salt and pepper			

method

1. Cook the tortellini for 13-15 minutes, according to the instructions on the packet.

2. Meanwhile melt the butter in a saucepan. Add the onions, garlic and mushrooms and cook gently for 5 minutes.

3. Add the crême fraiche and herbs. Season with salt and pepper.

4. Drain the cooked tortellini and stir into the sauce.

15 min Preparation time
15 min Cooking time

Puddings

Eating some fresh fruit is the best way to finish your meal - but for those who have a sweet tooth and are not on a diet, here are a few quick and easy puds.

PANCAKES

The amounts given below are enough for 6-8 pancakes. Once you have made the pancakes, they can be stored for a week in the fridge (or they can be frozen), so it is a good idea to make more than you need for one meal. You might, for example, have sweet pancakes for pudding one day, and do savoury pancakes for a main meal the next.

To reheat the pancakes that you have stored in the fridge, put them between two plates on top of a pan of simmering water; or warm them under the grill.

ingredients	Metric	Imperial	American
Plain flour	100 g	4 oz	4 oz
Salt	pinch	pinch	pinch
Egg	1	1	1
Milk	300 ml	½ pint	1 ¼ cups
Oil or butter for cooking			

method

1. Sift the flour and salt into a mixing bowl, make a well in the centre and break the egg into it.

2. Using a wooden spoon, stir the egg and draw in the flour from around the side.

3. Gradually add just enough milk to incorporate all the flour and make a thick paste. Beat very well to remove all the lumps so that the mixture is smooth.

4. Stir in the remaining milk, a little at a time. Beat the batter thoroughly until small air bubbles appear all over the surface.

5. Leave the batter to stand for up to an hour, if you have time.

6. When you are ready to make the pancakes, heat a frying pan until it is really hot. Put in ½ teaspoon of oil or a small knob of butter and allow this to spread all around the pan.

7. Pour in a little batter and tilt the pan so that it runs all over the base - it should make a very thin layer.

8. Let the pancake cook for about 1 minute, shaking the pan a little to stop it sticking, until the top is just set and the underneath is lightly browned.

9. Use a fish slice or spatula to turn the pancake over and cook for about another 20 seconds until the other side is browned.

10. Turn the pancake out onto a plate and sprinkle with sugar and lemon juice; or spoon on some syrup, honey or jam.

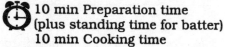 10 min Preparation time
(plus standing time for batter)
10 min Cooking time

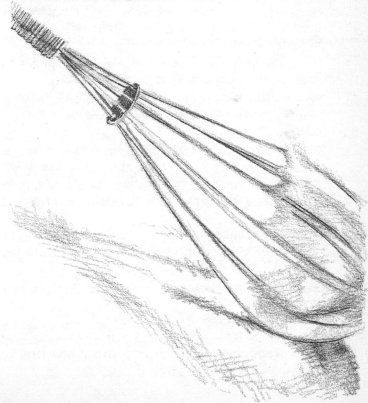

FRUIT FRITTERS

For fritters, make batter in the same way as for pancakes (page 88), but use half the amount of milk so that the batter is thicker.

ingredients	Metric	Imperial	American
Thick batter	300 ml	1 ½ pint	1 ¼ cups
Cooking apple, or			
a banana, or pineapple			
rings from a tin	1	1	1
Oil for frying			

method

1. Peel the apple, remove the core and slice into rings. (Or slice the banana in half lengthways, then in half across to make four pieces; or drain the pineapple rings from the tin.)

2. Pour about 1 cm/½ in oil into a frying pan and heat until a faint smoke is rising from it.

3. Dip the pieces of fruit in the batter so that they are thickly coated, and then lower them into the hot oil.

4. Fry the fritters until they are a deep golden brown, then lift out with a fish slice and drain on kitchen paper.

5. Sprinkle with sugar while still hot.

10 min Preparation time
(plus standing time for batter)
10 min Cooking time

FRIED BANANA

ingredients	Metric	Imperial	American
Banana	1	1	1
Butter	12.5 g	½ oz	½ oz
Honey or syrup			
Chopped nuts			

method

1. Peel the banana and cut in half lengthways.

2. Melt the butter in a frying pan and gently fry the banana until soft.

3. Lift out onto a serving plate. Spoon over some honey or syrup and top with chopped nuts.

5 - 10 min Preparation time
5 - 10 min Cooking time

CHOCOLATE PUDDING

(2 servings)

This is almost as quick and easy to make as the synthetic whips that you buy in a packet - and it tastes much better. Eat half of it warm, with a little cream, and the second helping will keep in the fridge to eat cold the following day.

ingredients	Metric	Imperial	American
Cornflour	25 g	1 oz	1 oz
Cocoa powder	25 g	1 oz	1 oz
Sugar	25 g	1 oz	1 oz
Milk	300 ml	½ pint	1 ¼ cups

method

1. Put the cornflour, cocoa powder and sugar into a small basin and stir in enough milk to make a thinnish paste. Make sure the ingredients are really well mixed, particularly the cornflour.

2. Pour the remaining milk into a small saucepan and heat until almost boiling.

3. Stir the hot milk into the chocolate mixture.

4. Mix well and pour the whole lot back into the saucepan.

5. Cook on a moderate heat, stirring continuously, until the mixture is boiling and has thickened.

6. Remove from the heat and pour back into the basin.

7. Sprinkle a little sugar on top to prevent a skin forming.

8. Eat warm or cold, with a little cream.

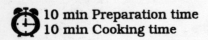 10 min Preparation time
10 min Cooking time

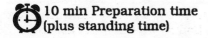

SUMMER PUDDING

(2 servings)

This is a handy way of using up some not-too-fresh bread. Use fresh, tinned, bottled or frozen raspberries, blackberries or redcurrants. The pudding needs to stand for 24 hours to allow the fruit juices to soak into the bread.

ingredients	Metric	Imperial	American
Soft fruit	*450 g*	*1 lb*	*1 lb*
Sugar (if using fresh fruit)	*25 g*	*1 oz*	*1 oz*
Thin slices of bread	*4-5*	*4-5*	*4-5*

method

1. If you are using fresh fruit, stew it with sugar in a little water.

2. Cut the crusts off the bread and line a bowl so that the slices fit closely together.

3. Put in the fruit.

4. Lay more bread on top so that the fruit is completely covered.

5. Put a plate with a weight on it on top of the pudding and leave for 24 hours.

10 min Preparation time
(plus standing time)

ZABAGLIONE

Make this delicious dessert when you want a special treat!

ingredients	Metric	Imperial	American
Egg yolk	1	1	1
Sweet sherry or marsala	15 ml	1 tbsp	1 tbsp
Castor sugar	25 g	1 oz	1 oz
Sponge fingers			

method

1. Put the egg yolk, sherry and sugar into a bowl. Set the bowl over a pan of hot water on the stove.

2. Whisk the mixture until it becomes thick and creamy.

3. Spoon into a glass and eat immediately, accompanied by sponge fingers.

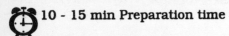 10 - 15 min Preparation time

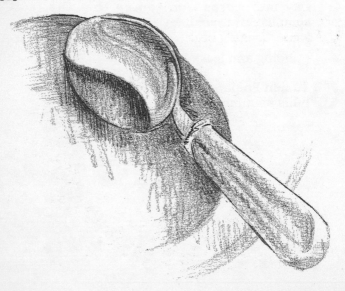

FRESH FRUIT SALAD

Use whatever fresh fruit you have available - apple, orange, pear, grapes, kiwi fruit, and so on. Sliced banana should be added just before serving.

ingredients	Metric	Imperial	American
Fresh fruit	*225 g*	*8 oz*	*8 oz*
Water	*300 ml*	*½ pint*	*1¼ cups*
Sugar	*40-50g*	*1½-2 oz*	*1½-2 oz*
Lemon juice	*15 ml*	*1 tbsp*	*1 tbsp*

method

1. Put the water and sugar into a small saucepan and boil for 5 minutes. Add the lemon juice.

2. Prepare the fruit according to its kind - peel, core and slice apples and pears; divide oranges into segments, and so on.

3. Put the prepared fruit into a dish and pour over the syrup. Cover the bowl and leave to become cold.

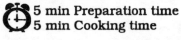
5 min Preparation time
5 min Cooking time

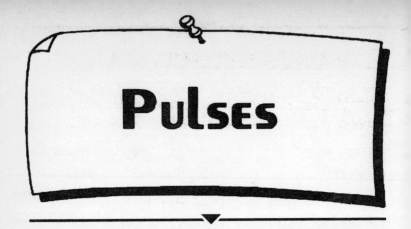

Pulses

Pulses, dried beans and peas, have become much more popular recently as people appreciate their nutritional value. Pulses contain valuable protein, which makes them ideal for vegetarians, as well as important vitamins and minerals such as vitamin B, iron and phosphorus. They are also high in fibre, and contain no saturated fat.

Supermarkets now stock a wide range of both dried and canned beans. The dried ones are cheaper, but they require more effort because most of them need to be soaked for several hours and then cooked before using them. If you are eating on your own it's much easier to open a small tin.

The amounts given in the following recipes make really large meals. Unless you have an enormous appetite, save half for the following day - it tastes even better when reheated.

All of these dishes are suitable for vegetarians, with rice or bread.

SPICY CHICK PEAS WITH TOMATO

ingredients	Metric	Imperial	America
Tin chick peas	200 g	7 oz	7oz
Vegetable oil	15 ml	1 tbsp	1 tbsp
Small onion, peeled and sliced	1	1	1
Clove of garlic, crushed	1	1	1
Turmeric	2.5 ml	½ tsp	½ tsp
Paprika	2.5 ml	½ tsp	½ tsp
Ground cumin	2.5 ml	½ tsp	½ tsp
Ground coriander	2.5 ml	½ tsp	½ tsp
Garam masala	2.5 ml	½ tsp	½ tsp
Tomatoes, chopped	2	2	2
Salt and pepper			

method

1. Drain the chick peas through a sieve.

2. Heat the oil in a saucepan and fry the onion and garlic for about 5 minutes, until soft.

3. Add the spices and continue cooking for another 2 minutes, stirring all the time.

4. Add the tomatoes and continue cooking until they are soft.

5. Add the chick peas, stir well, and cook for another 5 minutes.

6. Season with salt and pepper.

20 min Preparation time
20 min Cooking time

CHICK PEA STEW

ingredients	Metric	Imperial	American
Tin chick peas	200 g	7 oz	7 oz
Cooking oil	15 ml	1 tbsp	1 tbsp
Small onion, peeled and sliced	1	1	1
Clove of garlic, crushed	1	1	1
Green pepper, sliced	½	½	½
Red pepper, sliced	½	½	½
Salt and pepper			
Natural yoghurt	30 ml	2 tbsp	2 tbsp

method

1. Drain the chick peas through a sieve.

2. Heat the oil in a saucepan and gently fry the onion and garlic for 2-3 minutes, until soft.

3. Add the peppers and cook for another 2-3 minutes.

4. Add the drained chick peas, and season with salt and pepper. Simmer gently for 10 minutes.

5. Stir in the yoghurt and continue cooking for a couple of minutes until the stew has thickened.

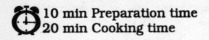 10 min Preparation time
20 min Cooking time

CHICK PEA CURRY

ingredients	Metric	Imperial	American
Tin chick peas	200 g	7 oz	7 oz
Cooking oil	15 ml	1 tbsp	1 tbsp
Small onion, peeled and sliced	1	1	1
Curry powder	5 ml	1 tsp	1 tsp
Tin tomatoes	200 g	7 oz	7 oz
Natural yoghurt (optional)	30 ml	2 tbsp	2 tbsp

method

1. Drain the chick peas through a sieve.

2. Heat the oil in a saucepan and gently fry the onion for about 5 minutes, until soft.

3. Add the curry powder and cook for another minute, stirring continuously.

4. Add the tinned tomatoes and drained chick peas. Continue cooking for another 5 minutes, until everything is heated through.

5. Add the yoghurt just before eating.

15 min Preparation time
15 min Cooking time

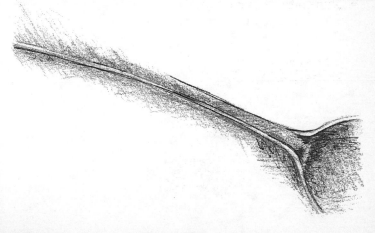

LENTIL CURRY

ingredients	Metric	Imperial	American
Red lentils	½ cup	½ cup	½ cup
Cooking oil	15 ml	1 tbsp	1 tbsp
Small onion, peeled and sliced	1	1	1
Curry powder	5 ml	1 tsp	1 tsp
Tomato purée	15 ml	1 tbsp	1 tbsp
Small potato, diced	1	1	1
Carrot, diced	1	1	1
Button mushrooms, sliced	50 g	2 oz	2 oz
Peas, frozen or tinned	50 g	2 oz	2 oz

method

1. Heat the oil in a saucepan and gently fry the onions and lentils for 5 minutes.

2. Add just enough water to cover the lentils and continue cooking for a further 10-15 minutes until the water is absorbed.

3. Add the curry powder and tomato purée, and stir well.

4. Add the vegetables and a little more water.

5. Cover and simmer for another 10-15 minutes, until the vegetables are cooked.

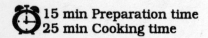 15 min Preparation time
25 min Cooking time

MEXICAN BEANS

Depending on what kind of vegetarian you are, the cheese in this dish is optional.

ingredients	Metric	Imperial	American
Tin red kidney beans	200 g	7 oz	7 oz
Cooking oil	15 ml	1 tbsp	1 tbsp
Small onion, peeled and thinly sliced	1	1	1
Tin tomatoes	200 g	7 oz	7 oz
Salt and pepper			
Grated cheddar cheese (optional)	25 g	1 oz	1 oz

method

1. Drain the beans into a sieve and rinse thoroughly under the cold tap.

2. Heat the oil in a saucepan and fry the onion gently for 5 minutes.

3. Add the tomatoes and continue cooking for another 5 minutes.

4. Add the drained beans. Season with salt and pepper. Simmer over a low heat for 20 minutes.

5. If you are adding cheese, stir it in just before eating.

10 min Preparation time
30 min Cooking time

CHILLI BEANS

ingredients	Metric	Imperial	American
Tin red kidney beans	200 g	7 oz	7 oz
Cooking oil	15 ml	1 tbsp	1 tbsp
Small onion, peeled and sliced	1	1	1
Small green or red pepper, sliced	1	1	1
Chilli powder	2.5 ml	½ tsp	½ tsp
Dried mixed herbs	2.5 ml	½ tsp	½ tsp
Tomato purée	5 ml	1 tsp	1 tsp
Salt and pepper			

method

1. Drain the beans into a sieve and rinse thoroughly under the cold tap.

2. Heat the oil in a saucepan and gently fry the onion and pepper for 5 minutes.

3. Add the beans and the rest of the ingredients and cook for another 10 minutes.

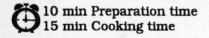 10 min Preparation time
15 min Cooking time

Bean and Pasta Stew

ingredients	Metric	Imperial	American
Tin cannellini or borlotti beans	200 g	7 oz	7 oz
Cooking oil	15 ml	1 tbsp	1 tbsp
Small onion, peeled and sliced	1	1	1
Clove of garlic, crushed	1	1	1
Tin tomatoes	200 g	7 oz	7 oz
Tomato purée	15 ml	1 tbsp	1 tbsp
Pasta shapes	50 g	2 oz	2 oz
Dried herbs	5 ml	1 tsp	1 tsp

method

1. Drain the beans through a sieve.

2. Heat the oil in a saucepan and fry the onion and garlic for 2-3 minutes.

3. Add the beans, tomatoes and tomato purée and cook for another 2 minutes.

4. Add the pasta and dried herbs. Simmer gently for 7-8 minutes, until the pasta is cooked.

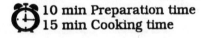
10 min Preparation time
15 min Cooking time

CANNELLINI BEANS WITH COURGETTE AND MUSHROOMS

This dish is also excellent cold. Eat half of it hot with rice or pasta, and keep the rest in the refrigerator overnight to eat the following day as a salad with French bread.

ingredients	Metric	Imperial	American
Tin cannellini beans	*200 g*	*7 oz*	*7 oz*
Water	*½ cup*	*½ cup*	*½ cup*
Tomato purée	*15 ml*	*1 tbsp*	*1 tbsp*
Olive or sunflower oil	*15 ml*	*1 tbsp*	*1 tbsp*
Wine vinegar	*15 ml*	*1 tbsp*	*1 tbsp*
Clove of garlic, crushed	*1*	*1*	*1*
Ground coriander	*pinch*	*pinch*	*pinch*
Salt and pepper			
Small onion, peeled and chopped	*1*	*1*	*1*
Small courgette, sliced	*1*	*1*	*1*
Button mushrooms, sliced	*50 g*	*2 oz*	*2 oz*
Parsley, chopped (optional)	*15 ml*	*1 tbsp*	*1 tbsp*

method

1. Drain the cannellini beans through a sieve.

2. Put the water, tomato purée, oil, vinegar, garlic, coriander, salt and pepper into a saucepan. Bring to the boil, then simmer for 5 minutes.

3. Add the onion, courgette, and mushrooms and cook for 3-5 minutes, until the vegetables are just cooked but still crunchy.

4. Add the drained beans and parsley. Heat through for another minute.

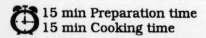
15 min Preparation time
15 min Cooking time

104

BEAN GOULASH

For this simple goulash use whichever tins of beans you have in your store cupboard. Eaten with pitta bread this is a nourishing and filling quick meal for a cold day. If there is too much for one meal, it will reheat nicely.

ingredients	Metric	Imperial	American
Oil	*10 ml*	*2 tsp*	*2tsp*
Small onion, peeled and sliced	*1*	*1*	*1*
Clove of garlic, crushed (optional)	*1*	*1*	*1*
Paprika	*5-10 ml*	*1-2 tsp*	*1-2 tsp*
Tin red kidney beans	*200 g*	*7 oz*	*7 oz*
Tin borlotti or butter beans	*200 g*	*7 oz*	*7 oz*
Tin tomatoes	*200 g*	*7 oz*	*7 oz*
Salt and pepper			

method

1. Heat the oil in a saucepan and fry the onion and garlic for 3-4 minutes.

2. Add the paprika and cook for another minute.

3. Rinse and drain the beans and add to the pan with the tomatoes.

4. Simmer gently for 5 minutes until all the ingredients are heated through.

5. Season to taste.

6. Serve with pitta bread.

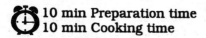 10 min Preparation time
10 min Cooking time

Rice

Rice goes well with many dishes, and there is never the problem of having to buy more than you need because it will keep for ages in a glass jar or plastic container. Ordinary long grain rice is perfectly all right for the recipes in this book, but now that there are so many different varieties available you could be more adventurous. Italian risotto rice is more starchy than long grain, and is best for making a genuinely creamy risotto. Basmati rice, which has long thin pointed grains, goes well with curries and is good for making fried rice. Brown, or wholegrain, rice has not been refined like white rice. It contains more natural nutrients and has a pleasant nutty flavour - but takes twice as long to cook.

Everybody has their own method for cooking rice. Here are two methods that should produce perfect rice every time.

Time saver tip
Cook double the amount of rice and keep half for a rice salad (page 125), rice omelette (page 35), kedgeree (page 49) or cheesy rice (page 14).

TO BOIL RICE

method 1

1. Bring to the boil a saucepan of water - you can speed this up by heating the water in a kettle first.

2. When the water is boiling, add the rice and half a teaspoon of salt.

3. Bring back to the boil, and then lower the heat a little so that the rice is boiling fairly rapidly but without spilling over the edges.

4. Boil for 12-15 minutes (25-30 minutes for brown rice) until the rice is soft. To test if the rice is cooked squeeze a grain between your thumb and forefinger. If it is not properly cooked there will be a hard particle of starch in the centre of each grain. When cooked the rice will be quite soft.

5. Drain the cooked rice into a sieve and rinse under hot water to remove excess starch and separate the grains.

6. Put about 1 cm/½ inch of water in the bottom of a saucepan, bring it to the boil and then reduce the heat so that the water continues to steam.

7. Rest the sieve containing the rice on top of the saucepan and steam it for 10 minutes - by which time the rice will be nice and fluffy, with the grains separated.

method 2

The important thing to remember with this method is that the ratio of water to rice is 2:1.

1. Measure two small cups of water into a saucepan and bring to the boil.

2. Add one small cup of rice and half a teaspoon of salt.

3. Bring back to the boil, then reduce the heat to the lowest possible setting, cover the pan with a lid and simmer for 20 minutes (40 minutes for brown rice).

4. Turn off the heat and leave for 5-10 minutes without lifting the lid.

SPICED RICE

This goes particularly well with kebabs and other skewered food.

ingredients	Metric	Imperial	American
Butter	12.5 g	½ oz	½ oz
Small onion, peeled and finely chopped	1	1	1
Ground cinnamon	pinch	pinch	pinch
Ground cumin	pinch	pinch	pinch
Ground turmeric	2.5 ml	½ tsp	½ tsp
Water	2 cups	2 cups	2 cups
Long-grain rice	1 cup	1 cup	1 cup
Salt and black pepper			

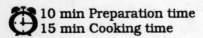

method

1. Melt the butter in a saucepan and gently fry the onion until soft.

2. Add the spices and continue cooking for another minute.

3. Add the water, rice, salt and pepper. Bring to the boil, then reduce the heat to simmering point. Simmer gently for 12-15 minutes, until all the water has been absorbed and the rice is soft.

10 min Preparation time
15 min Cooking time

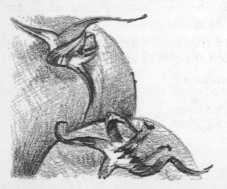

CHICKEN PILAFF

ingredients	Metric	Imperial	American
Boiling water	2 cups	2 cups	2 cups
Chicken stock cube	1	1	1
Butter	25 g	1 oz	1 oz
Small onion, peeled and sliced	1	1	1
Cooked chicken	75g	3 oz	3 oz
Rice	1 cup	1 cup	1 cup
Tomato, chopped	1	1	1
Dried thyme	¼ tsp	¼ tsp	¼ tsp
Salt and pepper			

method

1. Put the rice into a sieve and rinse it thoroughly under cold water until the water runs clear. Leave to drain.

2. Dissolve the stock cube in the boiling water.

3. Heat the butter in a saucepan and gently fry the onion until it is transparent.

4. Cut the cooked chicken into strips and add to the saucepan. Fry until it is light brown.

5. Add the rice and continue cooking for 2 minutes, stirring continuously to stop it sticking to the pan.

6. Add the tomato, chicken stock, thyme, salt and pepper.

7. Bring to the boil, then reduce the heat until the liquid is simmering gently.

8. Simmer for 12-15 minutes, until all the water has been absorbed and the rice is soft.

9. Serve with a green salad.

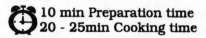
10 min Preparation time
20 - 25min Cooking time

HAM RISOTTO

The difference between a pilaff and a risotto is that in a pilaff the rice is dry, but in a real Italian risotto it is rich and creamy. Ideally, a risotto should be made with short-grain Italian rice, but you can use long grain.

ingredients	Metric	Imperial	American
Italian risotto rice	*1 cup*	*1 cup*	*1 cup*
Boiling water	*2 cups*	*2 cups*	*2 cups*
Stock cube	*1*	*1*	*1*
Cooking oil	*15 ml*	*1 tbsp*	*1 tbsp*
Small onion, peeled and sliced	*1*	*1*	*1*
Green pepper, sliced	*½*	*½*	*½*
Cooked ham	*75 g*	*3 oz*	*3 oz*
Tomato	*1*	*1*	*1*
Salt and pepper			
Cheddar cheese, grated	*25 g*	*1 oz*	*1 oz*

method

1. Dissolve the stock cube in the boiling water.

2. Heat the oil in a saucepan and fry the onion and pepper until they are soft.

3. Cut the ham into strips or cubes and add to the saucepan. Fry gently for another 2 minutes.

4. Add the rice and cook, stirring continuously, for another 2 minutes.

5. Add the tomato and stir in the stock. Season with salt and pepper.

6. Bring to the boil and then reduce the heat until the liquid is simmering gently.

7. Simmer for 12-15 minutes, until all the liquid is absorbed and the rice is soft.

8. Sprinkle with grated cheese before eating and serve with a green salad.

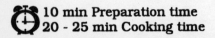 10 min Preparation time
20 - 25 min Cooking time

HAM FRIED RICE

ingredients	Metric	Imperial	American
Cooking oil	15 ml	1 tbsp	1 tbsp
Egg, beaten	1	1	1
Cooked rice	1 cup	1 cup	1 cup
Salt			
Cooked ham, chopped	50 g	2 oz	2 oz
Small tin shrimps, drained	1	1	1
Soy sauce	5 ml	1 tsp	1 tsp
Spring onions, chopped	2-3	2-3	2-3
Lettuce leaves, shredded	2-3	2-3	2-3

method

1. Heat the oil in a frying pan or wok and pour in the beaten egg. When it is half set, mix in the cooked rice and add salt to taste.

2. Add the chopped ham and drained shrimps and continue to fry for 5 minutes.

3. Sprinkle with soy sauce and mix in the chopped onions.

4. Spoon the fried rice onto a plate and arrange the shredded lettuce around the edge.

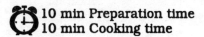 10 min Preparation time
10 min Cooking time

TUNA FRIED RICE

ingredients	Metric	Imperial	American
Cooking oil	15 ml	1 tbsp	1 tbsp
Small onion, peeled and finely sliced	1	1	1
Cooked rice	1 cup	1 cup	1 cup
Salt and pepper			
Egg, beaten	1	1	1
Small tin tuna	100 g	3½ oz	3½ oz
Peas, cooked	25 g	1 oz	1 oz
Soy sauce	10 ml	2 tsp	2 tsp
Spring onions, chopped			

method

1. Heat half the oil in a frying pan or wok and fry the onion until transparent. Push to one side.

2. Put in the rice and cook for 5 minutes, turning frequently. Mix in with the onion and season to taste.

3. Make a well in the centre of the rice, pour in the rest of the oil and the beaten egg. Stir until the egg is almost scrambled and then mix into the rice and continue frying for 2 more minutes.

4. Drain and flake the tuna and add to the rice mixture with the peas and soy sauce. Cook for another couple of minutes.

5. Serve hot sprinkled with chopped spring onions.

15 min Preparation time
15 min Cooking time

VEGETABLE FRIED RICE

ingredients	Metric	Imperial	American
Cooking oil	15 ml	1 tbsp	1 tbsp
Clove of garlic, finely chopped	1	1	1
Small piece of root ginger, grated (or a pinch of ground ginger)			
Green pepper, diced	½	½	½
Button mushrooms, sliced	50 g	2 oz	2 oz
Peas, cooked	50 g	2 oz	2 oz
Tomato, chopped	1	1	1
Light soy sauce	15 ml	1 tbsp	1 tbsp
Cooked rice	1 cup	1 cup	1 cup

method

1. Heat the oil in a frying pan and fry the garlic and ginger for 1 minute.

2. Add the pepper, mushrooms, peas and tomato and fry for 4 minutes, stirring continuously.

3. Add the soy sauce and cooked rice and mix thoroughly.

4. Heat through for 2-3 minutes, adding more soy sauce if needed.

10 min Preparation time
10 min Cooking time

RICE AND BEANS

ingredients	Metric	Imperial	American
Cooking oil	15 ml	1 tbsp	1 tbsp
Ground pork	50 g	2 oz	2 oz
Small onion, peeled and sliced	1	1	1
Green chilli, seeded and chopped	½	½	½
Long grain rice	½ cup	½ cup	½ cup
Stock (made with a stock cube)	1 cup	1 cup	1 cup
Tomato, chopped	1	1	1
Salt and pepper			
Red kidney beans	50 g	2 oz	2 oz

method

1. Heat the oil in a saucepan and fry the pork and onion for 5 minutes.

2. Add the chilli and rice and fry for another 2 minutes, stirring continuously.

3. Add the stock and tomato. Season with salt and pepper. Bring to the boil, cover, and simmer for 10 minutes.

4. Add the beans, and a little extra water if the rice looks too dry. Cover and cook for 5 minutes, until the liquid is absorbed and the rice is soft.

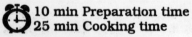
10 min Preparation time
25 min Cooking time

Spinach and Mushroom Risotto

This an excellent dish for vegetarians, and really is much better if you use Italian risotto rice (Arborio).

ingredients	Metric	Imperial	American
Olive oil	10 ml	2 tsp	2 tsp
Small onion, peeled and finely chopped	1	1	1
Italian risotto rice	50 g	2 oz	2 oz
Vegetable stock	300 ml	10 fl oz	1¼ cups
Mushrooms, chopped	100 g	4 oz	4 oz
Spinach, fresh or frozen	75 g	3 oz	3 oz
Lemon juice	5 ml	1 tsp	1 tsp
Salt and pepper			
Grated nutmeg	pinch	pinch	pinch
Parmesan cheese (optional)			

method

1. Heat the oil in a saucepan and add the chopped onion. Cook gently until the onion is softened.

2. Stir in the rice, and after cooking for 1 minute add the stock. Bring to the boil and simmer for about 10 minutes, until almost all the stock has been absorbed.

3. Add the mushroom and spinach, with a teaspoon of lemon juice. Cook for a further 2-3 minutes, stirring occasionally.

4. Season with salt, pepper and a pinch of nutmeg.

5. To serve, sprinkle with Parmesan cheese.

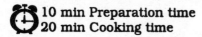
10 min Preparation time
20 min Cooking time

PRAWN FRIED RICE

This is a good way of using up some cooked, leftover rice.

ingredients	Metric	Imperial	American
Cooking oil	15 ml	1 tbsp	1 tbsp
Small onion, peeled and chopped	1	1	1
Clove of garlic, crushed	1	1	1
Sesame seeds	10 ml	2 tsp	2 tsp
Red pepper, chopped	½	½	½
Mushrooms, chopped	25 g	1 oz	1 oz
Frozen peas	15 ml	1 tbsp	1 tbsp
Soy sauce	15 ml	1 tbsp	1 tbsp
Prawns, tinned or frozen	50 g	2 oz	2 oz
Black pepper			
Cooked rice	1 cup	1 cup	1 cup
Egg, beaten	1	1	1

method

1. Heat the oil in a frying pan or wok. Add the onion, garlic, sesame seeds, red pepper and mushrooms. Cook gently for 10 minutes.

2. Add the peas, soy sauce and prawns. Season with black pepper. Continue cooking for 5 minutes.

3. Add the cooked rice, stirring well to mix the ingredients.

4. Make a well in the centre of the mixture, pour in the beaten egg and cook for a couple of minutes on a high heat. Stir well as the egg scrambles.

10 min Preparation time
20 min Cooking time

CURRIED RICE

Use up leftover cooked meat - chicken, pork or beef - in this quick rice dish. Flaked cooked fish could be used in place of meat.

ingredients	Metric	Imperial	American
Small onion, peeled and sliced	*1*	*1*	*1*
Margarine or butter	*12 g*	*½ oz*	*½ oz*
Curry powder	*5 ml*	*1 tsp*	*1 tsp*
Long grain rice	*½ cup*	*½ cup*	*½ cup*
Water	*1 cup*	*1 cup*	*1 cup*
Salt	*pinch*	*pinch*	*pinch*
Cooked meat, diced	*50 g*	*2 oz*	*2 oz*
Sultanas	*15 ml*	*1 tbsp*	*1 tbsp*
Desiccated coconut	*15 ml*	*1 tbsp*	*1 tbsp*
Hardboiled egg	*1*	*1*	*1*

method

1. Melt the margarine in a saucepan and gently fry the onion until soft.

2. Stir in the curry powder and cook for another minute.

3. Add the rice, water and salt. Bring to the boil and cook for about 12 minutes, until the rice is soft and the water has been absorbed. .

4. Add the cooked meat, sultanas and coconut.

5. Spoon onto a plate. Slice the hardboiled egg and arrange on top.

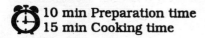 10 min Preparation time
15 min Cooking time

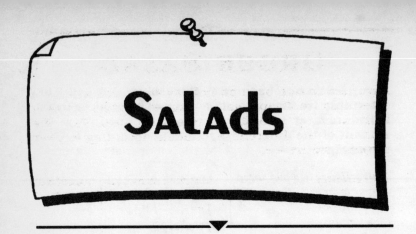

Salads

The salads described here are complete meals in themselves. Eaten with some good, crusty bread they make an ideal summer lunch or supper. Keep some fresh salad ingredients in the vegetable drawer of the refrigerator - plus a few tins and packets in the store cupboard - and you will always have the basic ingredients of a healthy, instant meal. Leftover cooked pasta, rice or potatoes can always be used as part of a salad, so it's a good idea to cook a little extra, ready for the next meal.

GREEK SALAD

Anyone who has been on holiday to Greece will have eaten this traditional salad - served in tavernas as a light lunch, or as a starter to a main meal. Vary the amount of the different ingredients according to your personal preference.

ingredients	Metric	Imperial	American
Lettuce leaves	*3-4*	*3-4*	*3-4*
Ripe tomatoes	*2*	*2*	*2*
Small, sweet cucumber	*½*	*½*	*½*
Black olives	*6*	*6*	*6*
Feta cheese	*50 g*	*2 oz*	*2 oz*
Olive oil	*15 ml*	*1 tbsp*	*1 tbsp*
Wine vinegar or lemon juice	*10 ml*	*2 tsp*	*2 tsp*
Fresh chopped herbs	*5 ml*	*1 tsp*	*1 tsp*

method

1. Wash the lettuce leaves, tear or shred them and arrange on a plate.

2. Chop the tomatoes and cucumber and arrange on top of the lettuce.

3. Add olives and cubes of feta cheese.

4. Mix the dressing ingredients together and pour over the salad.

 10 min Preparation time

SWISS SALAD

ingredients	Metric	Imperial	American
Gruyère cheese	50 g	2 oz	2 oz
Cooked ham	1 slice	1 slice	1 slice
Cooked boiled potatoes	2-3	2-3	2-3
Lettuce leaves	2-3	2-3	2-3
Natural yoghurt	30 ml	2 tbsp	2 tbsp
Mustard	½ tsp	½ tsp	½ tsp
Lemon juice	½ tsp	½ tsp	½ tsp
Salt and pepper			
Egg, hardboiled	1	1	1

method

1. Cut the cheese, ham and boiled potatoes into small cubes.

2. Chop the lettuce leaves finely.

3. Put these four ingredients into a bowl.

4. In another bowl mix together the yoghurt, mustard, lemon juice, and a little salt and pepper. Pour over the salad and toss lightly.

5. Cut the egg into wedges and arrange on top of the salad.

 10 min Preparation time

SALADE NIÇOISE

ingredients	Metric	Imperial	American
French beans	100 g	4 oz	4 oz
Olive oil	15 ml	1 tbsp	1 tbsp
Wine vinegar	10 ml	2 tsp	2 tsp
Salt and pepper			
Egg, hardboiled	1	1	1
Lettuce leaves	3	3	3
Spring onions, chopped	2	2	2
Tomato, quartered	1	1	1
Tin tuna fish	100 g	3½ oz	3 ½ oz
Anchovies (optional)			
Small green pepper, chopped	½	½	½
Black olives	6	6	6

method

1. Cut the beans in half (or leave them whole if they are small ones) and cook in boiling salted water for 5-7 minutes, until just tender. Drain into a colander and rinse under the cold tap.

2. Mix the beans with the oil, vinegar, salt and pepper and arrange on a plate.

3. Wash the lettuce leaves and arrange on top of the beans.

4. Shell and halve the hardboiled egg and arrange on top of the lettuce with the spring onions and tomato.

5. Turn the tuna fish into the centre.

6. Scatter anchovy fillets round the salad with chopped pepper and olives.

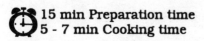 15 min Preparation time
5 - 7 min Cooking time

PASTA, BACON AND BEAN SALAD

ingredients	Metric	Imperial	American
Cooked pasta (quills or twirls)	100 g	4 oz	4 oz
Cooked beans, chopped	50 g	2 oz	2 oz
Streaky bacon, chopped	50 g	2 oz	2 oz
Olive oil	10 ml	2 tsp	2 tsp
Cider vinegar	5 ml	1 tsp	1 tsp
Mustard	2.5 ml	½ tsp	½ tsp
Honey	2.5 ml	½ tsp	½ tsp
Salt and pepper			
Chopped chives	10 ml	2 tsp	2 tsp

method

1. Cook the chopped bacon in a dry frying pan until it is crisp.

2. Remove from the heat and add the oil, mustard, vinegar and honey. Mix well and season to taste.

3. Add the cooked pasta and beans, and toss until everything is well mixed.

4. Sprinkle with chopped chives.

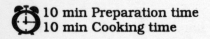

10 min Preparation time
10 min Cooking time

LOBIO

This bean salad is a Russian dish.

ingredients	Metric	Imperial	American
Tin red kidney beans	200 g	7 oz	7 oz
Clove of garlic, crushed	1	1	1
Small onion, peeled and finely chopped	1	1	1
Tomato, chopped	1	1	1
Chopped fresh herbs (or 5 ml/1 tsp dried herbs)	15 ml	1 tbsp	1 tbsp
Wine vinegar	15 ml	1 tbsp	1 tbsp
Oil	15 ml	1 tbsp	1 tbsp
Salt and pepper			
Feta cheese	50 g	2 oz	2 oz

method

1. Mix together the beans, garlic, onion, tomato and herbs.

2. Pour over the vinegar and oil.

3. Season with salt and pepper.

4. Crumble the feta cheese on top.

 10 min Preparation time

TUNA AND BUTTER BEAN SALAD

ingredients	Metric	Imperial	American
Lettuce leaves	3-4	3-4	3-4
Tin tuna fish	100 g	4 oz	4 oz
Tin butter beans	200 g	7 oz	7 oz
French dressing	15 ml	1 tbsp	1 tbsp

method

1. Wash the lettuce leaves and arrange them on a plate.

2. Drain and flake the tuna fish.

3. Drain the beans into a sieve and rinse well under cold water.

4. Mix the tuna fish and beans with the French dressing and spoon onto the lettuce leaves.

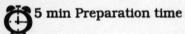 5 min Preparation time

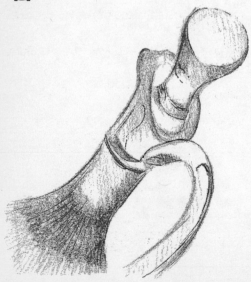

RICE AND CHICKEN SALAD

When you are cooking rice to serve with a meal, cook an extra portion to make this salad dish. Mix the rice while still warm with the oil and vinegar, so that it absorbs the flavours. Some chopped ham or tuna fish could be substituted for the chicken, and you could add or substitute some sweetcorn, beansprouts or cooked peas.

ingredients	Metric	Imperial	American
Cooked rice	75-100 g	3-4 oz	3-4 oz
Oil	15 ml	1 tbsp	1 tbsp
Wine vinegar	15 ml	1 tbsp	1 tbsp
Salt and pepper			
Cooked chicken, chopped	50-75 g	2-3 oz	2-3 oz
Button mushrooms, sliced	50 g	2 oz	2 oz
Green pepper, chopped	½	½	½
Tomato, sliced	1	1	1

method

1. While the rice is still warm, mix with the oil and vinegar, salt and pepper.

2. Just before you are ready to eat add the chicken and vegetables.

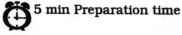 5 min Preparation time

CHICKEN, FRUIT AND PASTA SALAD

ingredients	Metric	Imperial	American
Pasta shapes	50-75 g	2-3 oz	2-3 oz
Olive oil	5 ml	1 tsp	1 tsp
Small eating apple, diced	1	1	1
Banana, sliced	½	½	½
Lemon juice	10 ml	2 tsp	2 tsp
Cooked chicken, cubed	50-75g	2-3 oz	2-3 oz
Walnuts, chopped	15 g	½ oz	½ oz
Mayonnaise	15 ml	1 tbsp	1 tbsp

method

1. Cook the pasta, drain and put into a bowl. Toss in the olive oil and leave to cool.

2. Put the apple and banana in a small bowl and sprinkle over the lemon juice.

3. Add the fruit to the cooled pasta, with the chicken and walnuts.

4. Stir in the mayonnaise.

5. Chill in the refrigerator before serving.

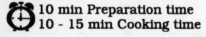 10 min Preparation time
10 - 15 min Cooking time

SALAMI, BEAN AND PASTA SALAD

ingredients	Metric	Imperial	American
Pasta shapes or macaroni	50 g	2 oz	2 oz
Salami, chopped	50 g	2 oz	2 oz
Red kidney beans (tinned or cooked dried ones)	50 g	2 oz	2 oz
Spring onions, chopped	2	2	2
Natural yoghurt	30 ml	2 tbsp	2 tbsp
Mustard	5 ml	1 tsp	1 tsp

method

1. Cook the pasta according to the instructions on the packet. Drain and leave to cool.

2. Put the cooked pasta into a bowl with the salami, beans and spring onions.

3. Mix the yoghurt and mustard together and stir into the salad ingredients.

4. Serve on a bed of lettuce, with crusty bread.

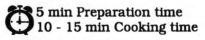

5 min Preparation time
10 - 15 min Cooking time

SALAD PARMENTIER

ingredients	Metric	Imperial	American
Egg	1	1	1
Cooked new potatoes	2-3	2-3	2-3
Cheddar cheese	50 g	2 oz	2 oz
Cooked ham	25 g	1 oz	1 oz
Mayonnaise	15 ml	1 tbsp	1 tbsp
Natural yoghurt	15 ml	1 tbsp	1 tbsp
Lemon juice	5 ml	1 tsp	1 tsp

method

1. Cook the egg in boiling water for about 8 minutes, until it is hardboiled. Put into cold water to cool, then remove the shell.

2. Chop the hardboiled egg, cooked potatoes, cheese and ham into small dice.

3. Mix the mayonnaise, yoghurt and lemon juice together. Stir into the egg and potato mixture.

4. Spoon the salad onto a bed of lettuce leaves and eat with crusty bread or a roll.

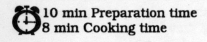 10 min Preparation time
8 min Cooking time

AVOCADO AND HAM SALAD

ingredients	Metric	Imperial	American
Avocado	1	1	1
Natural yoghurt	30 ml	2 tbsp	2 tbsp
Clove of garlic, crushed	1	1	1
Salt and pepper			
Cooked ham	50 g	2 oz	2 oz
Cheese, cubed	50 g	2 oz	2 oz
Red pepper, diced	½	½	½

method

1. Cut the avocado in half, remove the stone and scoop out the flesh.

2. Mix the avocado flesh with the yoghurt, crushed garlic, salt and pepper.

3. Add the cubed ham, cheese and red pepper to the avocado mixture.

4. Eat with granary or wholemeal bread.

 10 min Preparation time

FRENCH DRESSING FOR SALADS

Make enough French dressing to last a couple of weeks - shake well each time you use it.

ingredients	Metric	Imperial	American
Sunflower or olive oil	*60 ml*	*4 tbsp*	*4 tbsp*
Wine vinegar	*30 ml*	*2 tbsp*	*2 tbsp*
Castor sugar	*2.5 ml*	*½ tsp*	*½ tsp*
Dry mustard	*2.5 ml*	*½ tsp*	*½ tsp*
Salt and pepper			

method

1. Put all the ingredients into a screwtop jar.

2. Shake well before using.

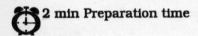 2 min Preparation time

SAUCES

Careful inspection of the supermarket shelves will
reveal all kinds of ready-made sauces in jars, tins and
packets. It's a good idea to keep a selection of these in
your store cupboard. A ready-made sauce poured over
pasta is one of the quickest and tastiest instant meals
there is. The sauces below are very simple to make
yourself, from ingredients that you are likely to have on
hand.

CURRY SAUCE

This curry sauce goes with eggs or leftover meat. It will keep in the refrigerator for a few days - or you can freeze it for future use. This is enough for two curries.

ingredients	Metric	Imperial	American
Onions, peeled and chopped	2	2	2
Apples, peeled and chopped	2	2	2
Butter or margarine	25 g	1 oz	1 oz
Flour	25 g	1 oz	1 oz
Curry powder	25 g	1 oz	1 oz
Curry paste (optional)	10 ml	2 tsp	2 tsp
Stock (made with stock cube)	600 ml	1 pint	2½ cups
Sultanas	25 g	1 oz	1 oz

method

1. Melt the butter or margarine in a saucepan and cook the onion and apple for 5 minutes, until soft.

2. Stir in the flour, curry powder and paste (if using) and cook for another 2 minutes.

3. Stir in the stock and bring to the boil.

4. Reduce the heat, add the sultanas, cover and simmer for 30 minutes.

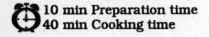 10 min Preparation time
40 min Cooking time

TOMATO SAUCE

This tomato sauce can be served with pasta, kebabs, meatballs - and anything else that needs livening up a bit. If you make more than you need for one meal, it will keep in the refrigerator for a week or so - or you can freeze some of it for future use.

ingredients	Metric	Imperial	American
Large ripe tomatoes	*2*	*2*	*2*
Water	*110 ml*	*4 fl oz*	*½ cup*
Worcestershire sauce	*2.5 ml*	*½ tsp*	*½ tsp*
Salt and pepper			
Garlic salt			

method

1   Make a slit in the skins of the tomatoes and put in boiling water until the skins start to peel. Remove the skins and chop the tomatoes.

2   Put the chopped tomatoes into a small saucepan with the water, Worcestershire sauce, and a pinch of salt, pepper and garlic salt.

3   Simmer until the tomatoes are reduced to a smooth purée.

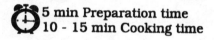 5 min Preparation time
10 - 15 min Cooking time

CHEESE SAUCE

Serve with fish or vegetables. This sauce is also the basis of cauliflower and macaroni cheese.

ingredients	Metric	Imperial	American
Butter or margarine	2.5 g	½ oz	½ oz
Flour	2.5 g	½ oz	½ oz
Milk	110 ml	4 fl oz	½ cup
Cheddar cheese, grated	25 g	1 oz	1 oz
Mustard	1.5 g	¼ tsp	¼ tsp
Salt and pepper			

method

1. Melt the butter in a saucepan and stir in the flour.

2. Remove the pan from the heat and gradually stir in the milk, making sure there are no lumps.

3. Return the pan to the heat and - still stirring - bring the sauce to the boil.

4. The sauce will now have thickened. Remove it from the heat and stir in the cheese, mustard, salt and pepper.

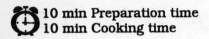
10 min Preparation time
10 min Cooking time

APPLE SAUCE

Apple sauce is traditionally served with roast pork (page 164), but it will also add interest to other meals. You can also add a little sugar and spoon it over ice cream as a dessert.

ingredients	Metric	Imperial	American
Cooking apple	*1*	*1*	*1*
Butter			
Water			

method

1. Peel and slice the apple and put into a small saucepan with a knob of butter and a couple of teaspoons of water.

2. Cook gently for 15-20 minutes, until the apple is soft.

3. Mash with a fork. Serve warm or cold.

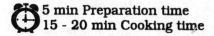 5 min Preparation time
15 - 20 min Cooking time

CHOCOLATE SAUCE

ingredients	Metric	Imperial	American
Cocoa powder	*15 ml*	*1 tbsp*	*1 tbsp*
Butter or margarine	*25 g*	*1 oz*	*1 oz*
Sugar	*25 g*	*1 oz*	*1 oz*

method

1. Put all the ingredients into a small saucepan and heat gently for 1-2 minutes, stirring all the time.

2. Serve hot, poured over ice cream, cooked pears, or other dessert.

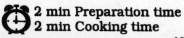 2 min Preparation time
2 min Cooking time

Soups

It is so tempting, when eating alone, just to open a tin of soup and leave it at that. Soup from a tin or packet is never substantial or nutritious enough to be a proper meal. These hearty soups, eaten with a hunk of fresh crusty bread and perhaps some cheese, are complete meals in themselves. They don't take much more effort than opening a tin, they taste ten times better, and they cost less. The amounts given are for two large servings, because soup will keep for a couple of days in the fridge. Make sure you bring it to the boil when you reheat it.

For some of the soups you need a liquidizer or a mouli-légumes. Either of these is a useful piece of equipment to have in your kitchen. A mouli-légumes works by hand and is much cheaper than a liquidizer. By attaching one of three different blades you can grate, mash or shred things into a bowl. It would also be useful for grating cheese, and vegetables for salads. You can push cooked vegetables through a sieve, but this is rather hard work.

ITALIAN BEAN AND PASTA SOUP

(2 servings)

ingredients	Metric	Imperial	American
Oil	10 ml	2 tsp	2 tsp
Small onion, peeled and chopped	1	1	1
Clove of garlic, crushed	1	1	1
Carrot, finely diced	1	1	1
Stick of celery, chopped	1	1	1
Tomato purée (paste)	5 ml	1 tsp	1 tsp
Beef stock	600 ml	1 pint	2½ cups
Tin borlotti beans	200 g	7 oz	7 oz
Small pasta shapes	25 g	1 oz	1 oz
Frozen or tinned peas	25 g	1 oz	1 oz
Salt			
Black pepper			

method

1. Heat the oil in a large saucepan. Add the onion, garlic, carrot and celery and cook gently for 5 minutes.

2. Add the tomato purée (paste), stock and beans.

3. Bring to the boil, cover and simmer for 10 minutes.

4. Add the pasta and peas and cook for a further 7 minutes, until the pasta is just cooked.

5. Add salt and pepper to taste.

10 min Preparation time
25 min Cooking time

MINESTRONE

(2 servings)

ingredients	Metric	Imperial	American
Oil	*10 ml*	*2 tsp*	*2 tsp*
Small onion, peeled and chopped	*1*	*1*	*1*
Clove of garlic, chopped	*1*	*1*	*1*
Carrot, chopped	*1*	*1*	*1*
Stalk of celery, chopped	*1*	*1*	*1*
Bacon, chopped	*25 g*	*1 oz*	*1 oz*
Stock or water	*600 ml*	*1 pint*	*2 ½ cups*
Small potato, peeled and diced	*1*	*1*	*1*
Courgette, chopped	*1*	*1*	*1*
Peas, tinned or frozen	*25 g*	*1 oz*	*1 oz*
Salt			
Black pepper			
Dried mixed herbs	*2.5 ml*	*½ tsp*	*½ tsp*
Tomato purée (paste)	*5 ml*	*1 tsp*	*1 tsp*
Rice or pasta	*25 g*	*1 oz*	*1 oz*

method

1. Heat the oil in a saucepan and gently cook the onion, garlic, carrot, celery and bacon until soft.

2. Add the stock or water, the rest of the vegetables, salt, pepper, herbs and tomato purée. Simmer for 25 minutes.

3. Add the rice or pasta and cook for a further 10 minutes.

4. Serve with grated Parmesan cheese.

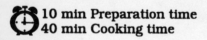 10 min Preparation time
40 min Cooking time

FRANKFURTER SOUP

(2 servings)

ingredients	Metric	Imperial	American
Butter or margarine	25 g	1 oz	1 oz
Small onion, peeled and chopped	1	1	1
Leek, washed and sliced	1	1	1
Potatoes, peeled and diced	2	2	2
Chicken stock (made with a stock cube)	450 ml	¾ pint	2 cups
Coriander seeds, or ground coriander	¼ tsp	¼ tsp	¼ tsp
Salt and pepper			
Milk	150 ml	¼ pint	⅔ cup
Frankfurter sausages, sliced	2	2	2

method

1. Melt the butter in a saucepan and gently fry the onion and leek for 5 minutes.

2. Add the diced potato, chicken stock and seasoning.

3. Bring to the boil, then reduce the heat, cover with a lid and simmer for 30 minutes.

4. Add the milk and frankfurters and continue simmering for another 10 minutes.

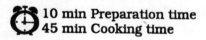 10 min Preparation time
45 min Cooking time

TOMATO AND PEPPERAMI SOUP

(2 servings)

ingredients	Metric	Imperial	American
Oil	10 ml	2 tsp	2 tsp
Small onion, peeled and chopped	1	1	1
Clove of garlic, crushed	1	1	1
Small red pepper, chopped	½	½	½
Tin chopped tomatoes	200 g	7 oz	7 oz
Beef stock	600 ml	1 pint	2 ½ cups
Worcestershire sauce	5 ml	1 tsp	1 tsp
Salt and pepper			
Small pepperami sausage, chopped			
Small pasta shapes	25 g	1 oz	1 oz

method

1. Heat the oil in a large saucepan. Add the onion, garlic and pepper and fry gently for 2 minutes.

2. Add the chopped tomatoes, half the beef stock and Worcestershire sauce. Season with salt and pepper.

3. Bring to the boil, cover and simmer for 15 minutes.

4. Blend in a liquidizer until smooth. (Or push through a sieve.)

5. Return the blended mixture to the pan and add the remaining stock, chopped sausage and pasta.

6. Bring to the boil, cover and simmer for 10 minutes.

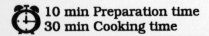

10 min Preparation time
30 min Cooking time

LENTIL, BACON AND TOMATO SOUP

(2 servings)

ingredients	Metric	Imperial	American
Bacon rashers, chopped	2	2	2
Oil	10 ml	2 tsp	2 tsp
Small onion, peeled and sliced	1	1	1
Large tomatoes, chopped	2	2	2
Chicken stock (made with stock cube)	600 ml	1 pint	2 ½ cups
Red lentils	50 g	2 oz	2 oz
Salt			
Black pepper			

method

1. Fry the bacon in a saucepan for 3-4 minutes, then lift out with a fish slice and keep aside.

2. In the same saucepan, heat the oil and gently fry the onion for 2-3 minutes.

3. Add the chopped tomatoes and stock. Bring to the boil, reduce the heat, cover with a lid and simmer for 45 minutes.

4. Put the soup into a liquidizer until smooth. (Or pour through a sieve into a bowl, pushing the lentils through with the back of a spoon and discarding any tomato skin that remains.)

5. Reheat the soup in the saucepan, and serve it with the cooked bacon sprinkled on top.

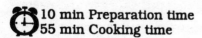
10 min Preparation time
55 min Cooking time

POTATO AND ONION SOUP

(1 serving)

This soup does not keep well, so the following ingredients are for only one serving.

ingredients	Metric	Imperial	American
Large onion, peeled and sliced	*1*	*1*	*1*
Large potato, peeled and cut into pieces	*1*	*1*	*1*
Carrot, sliced	*1*	*1*	*1*
Milk	*300 ml*	*½ pint*	*1¼ cups*
Salt and pepper			
Cheddar cheese, grated	*25 g*	*1 oz*	*1 oz*

method

1. Put the vegetables into a small saucepan and just cover them with water.

2. Bring to the boil, then reduce the heat, cover with a lid and simmer for 15 minutes, until the potatoes are soft.

3. Break the vegetables down a little with a fork (but do not mash them) and add the milk.

4. Season with salt and pepper.

5. Reheat, and sprinkle the grated cheese on top before eating.

🕐 10 min Preparation time
20 min Cooking time

TORTELLINI AND VEGETABLE SOUP

(2 servings)

Tortellini are little parcels of stuffed pasta - the stuffing might be something like beef and mortadella, or spinach and ricotto. Tortellini can be served with a sauce (see page 85), or added to soup.

ingredients	Metric	Imperial	American
Olive oil	15 ml	1 tbsp	1 tbsp
Spring onions, chopped	3	3	3
Carrot, finely chopped	1	1	1
Stick of celery, chopped	1	1	1
Clove of garlic, crushed	1	1	1
Smoked streaky bacon or chorizo chopped	25 g	1 oz	1 oz
Green lentils	25 g	1 oz	1 oz
Ham or chicken stock	675 ml	1¼ pint	3 cups
Salt and pepper			
Tortellini	40 g	1½ oz	1½ oz
Green vegetables - broccoli, courgettes or French beans	100 g	4 oz	4 oz

method

1. Heat the oil in a saucepan. Add the onions, carrot, celery, garlic, and bacon or chorizo. Cook over a moderate heat for 3-4 minutes.

2. Stir in the lentils and stock, salt and pepper. Bring to the boil, cover and simmer for 10 minutes.

3. Add the tortellini and simmer for 10 minutes.

4. Add the green vegetables and simmer for 5 minutes, or until the vegetables are tender.

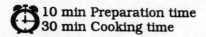
10 min Preparation time
30 min Cooking time

Stir-Fry

Stir-frying is a quick and easy way of cooking that is ideal if you are making a meal for one. It is based on the Chinese way of preparing food - vegetables and meat are chopped up into small pieces and cooked in oil over a very high heat, and you have to stir all the time to prevent them sticking or burning.

Because stir-fry dishes are cooked very quickly, you have to use tender, good quality meat. If you have time it is a good idea to leave the meat to marinate for half an hour or longer in some soy sauce or wine vinegar - this makes it more tender. Most vegetables are suitable. The trick is to have all the ingredients prepared - sliced, chopped or grated - and lined up in the order you are going to use them before you start the actual cooking. A wok is ideal for cooking stir-fry dishes, but if you don't have one a large non-stick frying pan will do. You will also need a really sharp knife and a chopping board as there is a lot of slicing and chopping involved.

Stir-fry dishes are usually served with rice (see page 106 for how to cook rice) or noodles.

BEEF STIR-FRY

ingredients	Metric	Imperial	American
Rump, sirloin or fillet steak	100 g	4 oz	4 oz
Cornflour	15 g	½ oz	½ oz
Chinese 5-spice powder	pinch	pinch	pinch
Soy sauce	15 ml	1 tbsp	1 tbsp
Sesame oil	15 ml	1 tbsp	1 tbsp
Fresh ginger, shredded	5 ml	1 tsp	1 tsp
Clove of garlic, chopped	1	1	1
Red pepper, thinly sliced	½	½	½
Broccoli florets	50 g	2 oz	2 oz
Spring onions, sliced	2-3	2-3	2-3
Sherry	15 ml	1 tbsp	1 tbsp
Water	15 ml	1 tbsp	1 tbsp

method

1. Cut the steak into very thin strips and put into a bowl with the cornflour, 5-spice powder and soy sauce. Mix well and leave to marinate for 30 minutes.

2. Heat the oil in a wok, add the marinated steak, ginger and garlic and stir-fry for 3-4 minutes.

3. Add the pepper, broccoli and spring onions and stir- fry for another 2 minutes.

4. Add the sherry and water, cover with a lid or plate, and cook for 1 minute.

5. Serve with rice.

10 min Preparation time
(plus 30 mins marinating time)
7 min Cooking time

STIR-FRIED PORK WITH STRING BEANS

The sweet bean paste in this recipe gives a distinctive flavour, but soy sauce may be used instead.

ingredients	Metric	Imperial	American
Lean pork	100 g	4 oz	4 oz
Soy sauce	10ml	2 tsp	2 tsp
Vegetable oil	15 ml	1 tbsp	1 tbsp
Fresh ginger, shredded	5 ml	1 tsp	1 tsp
Clove of garlic, crushed	1	1	1
Salt			
String beans	50 g	2 oz	2 oz
Small onion, sliced	1	1	1
Sweet bean paste	5 ml	1 tsp	1 tsp
Vegetable stock	15 ml	1 tbsp	1 tbsp
Cornflour	5 ml	1 tsp	1 tsp

method

1. Cut the pork into strips and put into a bowl with the soy sauce, half the oil, ginger, garlic and a pinch of salt. Leave to marinate for 10 minutes.

2. String the beans and cut into lengths the same size as the pork strips. Cook in salted water for 3 minutes and then drain, reserving some of the cooking liquid for stock.

3. Heat the remaining oil in a wok or frying pan and fry the onion for 1 minute. Remove with a slotted spoon and keep aside.

4. Add a little more oil to the wok if necessary and stir-fry the pork until it is browned.

5. Add the onion and string beans.

6. Mix the sweet bean paste with a tablespoon of reserved stock and blend in the cornflour. Add this to the pork and bean mixture and cook until the sauce is thickened.

7.   Serve with rice.

 10 min Preparation time
(plus 10 mins marinating time)
10 - 15 min Cooking time

STIR-FRIED SHRIMPS AND PEAS

ingredients	Metric	Imperial	American
Small frozen raw shrimps, defrosted	100 g	4 oz	4 oz
Cornflour	25 g	1 oz	1 oz
Salt	pinch	pinch	pinch
Egg white			
Sherry	15 ml	1 tbsp	1 tbsp
Cooking oil	15 ml	1 tbsp	1 tbsp
Fresh ginger, shredded	5 ml	1 tsp	1 tsp
Peas	25 g	1 oz	1 oz
Vegetable stock or water	15 ml	1 tbsp	1 tbsp
Sesame oil	1.5 ml	¼ tsp	¼ tsp

method

1. Put the defrosted shrimps into a bowl and sprinkle with half the cornflour and a pinch of salt. Stir in half an egg white and a tablespoon of sherry.

2. Heat the oil in a wok or frying pan and add the shredded ginger.

3. Add the prawns and stir-fry until they turn pink.

4. Add the peas and stir-fry for 3-4 minutes.

5. Blend the remaining cornflour with the stock and sesame oil and add this sauce to the pan.

6. Continue cooking for a couple of minutes until the sauce is slightly thickened and translucent.

7. Serve with rice or noodles.

10 min Preparation time
10 min Cooking time

SWEET AND SOUR PORK

ingredients	Metric	Imperial	American
Lean pork	100 g	4 oz	4 oz
Vinegar	15 ml	1 tbsp	1 tbsp
Soy sauce	15 ml	1 tbsp	1 tbsp
Small onion, chopped	1	1	1
Green pepper, chopped	½	½	½
Carrot, chopped	1	1	1
Sugar	5 ml	1 tsp	1 tsp
Tomato purée	5 ml	1 tsp	1 tsp
Pineapple juice	30 ml	2 tbsp	2 tbsp
Cornflour	5 ml	1 tsp	1 tsp
Water	15 ml	1 tbsp	1 tbsp
Cooking oil	15 ml	1 tbsp	1 tbsp
Salt and pepper			

method

1. Cut the pork into small cubes and put into a bowl with the vinegar and soy sauce. Mix thoroughly and leave to marinate for 30 minutes.

2. Prepare the vegetables.

3. When you are ready to stir-fry, lift the meat from the marinade with a slotted spoon. Stir the sugar, tomato purée, pineapple juice and cornflour mixed with water into the sauce left in the bowl.

4. Heat the oil in a wok or frying pan and when it is really hot add the pork and stir-fry for 3 minutes.

5. Add the vegetables. Stir-fry for 2 minutes.

6. Pour over the sauce and bring to the boil. Simmer for another couple of minutes.

10 min Preparation time
(plus 30 mins marinating time)
10 min Cooking time

BEEF STIR-FRY WITH NOODLES

ingredients	Metric	Imperial	American
Noodles	45g	3 oz	3 oz
Cooking oil	15 ml	1 tbsp	1 tbsp
Spring onions, chopped	2	2	2
Clove of garlic, crushed	1	1	1
Small carrot, cut into matchsticks	1	1	1
Green pepper, thinly sliced	½	½	½
Rump, sirloin or fillet steak	100 g	4 oz	4 oz
Beef stock	60 ml	4 tbsp	4 tbsp
Soy sauce	15 ml	1 tbsp	1 tbsp
Wine vinegar	10 ml	2 tsp	2 tsp
Cornflour	5 ml	1 tsp	1 tsp
Salt and pepper			
Sesame seeds	5 ml	1 tsp	1 tsp

method

1. Put the noodles into a saucepan of boiling water, remove from the heat and cover with a lid.

2. Meanwhile heat the oil in a frying pan or wok and stir-fry the onions, garlic, carrot and green pepper for 2-3 minutes.

3. Cut the meat into thin strips and add to the vegetables. Continue stir-frying for another 5-6 minutes, until the meat is browned and tender.

4. Add the stock, soy sauce and vinegar and bring to the boil. Blend the cornflour with a little cold water and stir into the sauce to thicken it.

5. Season with salt and pepper, and combine with the cooked noodles. Sprinkle with sesame seeds before serving.

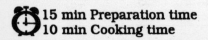 15 min Preparation time
10 min Cooking time

BACON STIR-FRY

ingredients	Metric	Imperial	American
Cooking oil	15 ml	1 tbsp	1 tbsp
Bacon, diced	50 g	2 oz	2 oz
Spring onions, chopped	2-3	2-3	2-3
Fresh ginger, shredded	5 ml	1 tsp	1 tsp
Carrot, cut into matchsticks	1	1	1
Baby sweetcorn	50 g	2 oz	2 oz
Broccoli florets	50 g	2 oz	2 oz
Button mushrooms, sliced	50 g	2 oz	2 oz
Light soy sauce	15 ml	1 tbsp	1 tbsp

method

1. Heat the oil in a wok or frying pan and fry the bacon until browned.

2. Add the onions and ginger and stir-fry for 1 minute.

3. Add the carrot, sweetcorn and broccoli and stir-fry for another 2-3 minutes.

4. Add the mushrooms and stir-fry for another 2-3 minutes, until the vegetables are tender but crisp.

5. Remove from the heat and stir in the soy sauce.

6. Serve with rice.

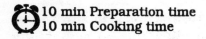10 min Preparation time
10 min Cooking time

CHICKEN AND PEPPERS

This dish looks more attractive if you use two or three different coloured peppers - but for one person it may be more economical to buy just one variety.

ingredients	Metric	Imperial	American
Boneless chicken breast	75-100 g	3-4 oz	3-4 oz
Red, yellow or green pepper			
(or a mixture)	1	1	1
Cloves of garlic	1	1	1
Soy sauce	15-30 ml	1-2 tbsp	1-2 tbsp

method

1. Remove the skin from the chicken and cut into bite-sized pieces. Remove the stalk and seeds from the pepper and cut into dice. Slice the garlic.

2. Heat the oil in a frying pan or wok. When it is really hot add the chicken and stir-fry for 4-5 minutes, until the flesh is white.

3. Turn down the heat to moderate. Push the chicken to one side of the pan and put the pepper and garlic on the other side. Continue cooking for 3-4 minutes, then mix chicken and pepper together and add the soy sauce.

4. Heat through for another couple of minutes.

5. Serve with rice.

10 min Preparation time
10 min Cooking time

CHICKEN CHOW MEIN

ingredients	Metric	Imperial	American
Skinned and boned chicken	75 g	3 oz	3 oz
Egg noodles	45 g	3 oz	3 oz
Cooking oil	15 ml	1 tbsp	1 tbsp
Small onion, peeled and sliced	1	1	1
Clove of garlic, sliced	1	1	1
Carrot, grated	1	1	1
Fresh beansprouts (or tinned)	150 g	6 oz	6 oz
Light soy sauce	15 ml	1 tbsp	1 tbsp
Sesame oil	5 ml	1 tsp	1 tsp
Sugar	1.5 ml	¼ tsp	¼ tsp
Salt	pinch	pinch	pinch

method

1 Slice the chicken into thin strips.

2 Put the noodles into a saucepan of boiling water, remove from the heat and cover with a lid. Put on one side.

3. Meanwhile heat the oil in a wok or frying pan, add the chicken and stir-fry for 2-3 minutes, until the chicken is white.

4. Add the onion, garlic and carrot, and stir-fry for another 2 minutes.

5. Add the beansprouts, soy sauce, sesame oil, sugar and salt.

6. Drain the noodles into a sieve and add to the chicken and beansprouts.

7. Mix everything together thoroughly and heat gently for a few minutes before serving.

10 min Preparation time
10 min Cooking time

CHICKEN WITH MUSHROOMS AND BROCCOLI

ingredients	Metric	Imperial	American
Boneless chicken breast	100 g	4 oz	4 oz
Cornflour	10 ml	2 tsp	2 tsp
Soy sauce	10 ml	2 tsp	2 tsp
Cooking oil	15 ml	1 tbsp	1 tbsp
Small onion, peeled and finely chopped	1	1	1
Clove of garlic, crushed	1	1	1
Broccoli, divided into florets	50 g	2 oz	2 oz
Button mushrooms	50 g	2 oz	2 oz
Sherry	30 ml	2 tbsp	2 tbsp
Salt and pepper			

method

1. Remove the skin from the chicken and cut into bite-sized pieces.

2. Put the cornflour into a small bowl and toss the chicken pieces in it.

3. Sprinkle the soy sauce over the chicken and leave to stand for 20 minutes.

4. Heat the oil in a large frying pan or wok and stir-fry the chicken for 2-3 minutes.

5. Push the chicken to one side, turn down the heat and add the onion and garlic. Cook for a further 2 minutes.

6. Add the broccoli florets and the mushrooms. Continue stir-frying these for a further minute, then mix all the ingredients together, drawing in the chicken from the side.

7. Pour over the sherry and heat through for another couple of minutes.

8. Serve with rice or noodles.

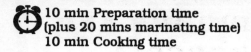 10 min Preparation time
(plus 20 mins marinating time)
10 min Cooking time

BEEF IN OYSTER SAUCE

This is equally good with black bean sauce - which has a spicier flavour.

ingredients	Metric	Imperial	American
Rump, sirloin or fillet steak	100 g	4 oz	4 oz
Green pepper	1	1	1
Cooking oil	15 ml	1 tbsp	1 tbsp
Oyster sauce	45 ml	3 tbsp	3 tbsp

method

1. Cut the steak into thin strips. Remove the stalk and seeds from the pepper and slice thinly.

2. Heat the oil in a frying pan or wok. When it is really hot add the sliced meat and cook for 3 minutes, stirring all the time.

3. Add the sliced pepper and continue frying for 2 more minutes.

4. Turn the heat down and add the oyster sauce. Heat through gently for a further 5 minutes.

5. Serve with rice.

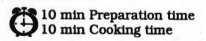 10 min Preparation time
10 min Cooking time

Three Meals In One

If you don't have much time during the week, but like to do some serious cooking at the weekend, here are some ideas for making three meals in one. Leftover meat should be wrapped in clingfilm and stored in the refrigerator for not more than a couple of days. Make sure it is thoroughly reheated.

THREE CHICKEN MEALS

Roast Chicken
Chicken Curry
Chicken á La King

ROAST CHICKEN WITH ROAST POTATOES

ingredients	Metric	Imperial	American
Whole chicken	1-1.5 kg	2-3 lb	2-3 lb
Bacon rashers, or oil and herbs			
Potatoes	2-4	2-4	2-4
Cooking fat	50 g	2 oz	2 oz

method

1. If the chicken was frozen, make sure that it is completely defrosted. Calculate the cooking time - 20 minutes per lb/450g, plus 20 minutes.

2. Preheat the oven to 400°F/200°C Gas Mark 6.

3. Place the chicken in an ovenproof dish. Either lay a couple of bacon rashers over the breast, or brush with oil and sprinkle with herbs.

4. Roast in the oven for the required time.

5. Put the cooking fat into another ovenproof dish and put it into the oven to heat up.

6. Meanwhile peel the potatoes and cut them into even-sized pieces. Bring to the boil in a saucepan of water and simmer for 2-3 minutes. Drain the potatoes and add them to the hot cooking fat.

7. Eat some of the chicken with the roast potatoes and some cooked vegetables.

8. When the chicken carcase is cool, remove the rest of the cooked chicken flesh. Wrap it in clingfilm and store in the fridge to use the following day in another recipe.

20 min Preparation time
1¼ hours Cooking time (depending on size of chicken)

CHICKEN CURRY

ingredients	Metric	Imperial	American
Cooked chicken	100 g	4 oz	4 oz
Butter or margarine	25 g	1 oz	1 oz
Onion, peeled and sliced	1	1	1
Curry powder	5 ml	1 tsp	1 tsp
Tin tomatoes	200 g	7 oz	7 oz

method

1. Melt the butter in a saucepan and cook the onion gently until it is soft and transparent.

2. Sprinkle the curry powder over the onion and stir. Cook for another minute.

3. Stir in the tomatoes, bring to the boil, then reduce the heat. Cover and simmer for 30 minutes.

4. Add the cooked chicken and continue simmering for another 10-15 minutes.

5. Eat with plain boiled rice.

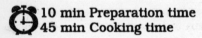 10 min Preparation time
45 min Cooking time

CHICKEN A LA KING

ingredients	Metric	Imperial	American
Cooked chicken	100 g	4 oz	4 oz
Butter	12.5 g	½ oz	½ oz
Small green pepper, sliced	½	½	½
Button mushrooms, sliced	4-5	4-5	4-5
Flour	12.5 g	½ oz	½ oz
Chicken stock (made with stock cube)	100 ml	4 fl oz	½ cup
Milk	30 ml	2 tbsp	2 tbsp
Salt and pepper			
Egg yolk	1	1	1
Natural yoghurt or cream	15 ml	1 tbsp	1 tbsp

method

1. Melt the butter in a saucepan and fry the green pepper gently for 2 minutes.

2. Add the mushrooms and fry for another 2 minutes.

3. Remove the pan from the heat and stir in the flour, then the stock and milk.

4. Return the pan to the heat and bring to the boil, stirring all the time as the sauce thickens.

5. Add the cooked chicken and season with salt and pepper. Heat through gently.

6. Stir the egg yolk into the yoghurt or cream, and then stir into the chicken mixture.

7. Continue heating gently for another minute or so, but do not allow it to boil.

8. Eat with plain boiled rice and a green salad.

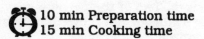
10 min Preparation time
15 min Cooking time

THREE MINCED BEEF MEALS

Cottage Pie
Spaghetti Bolognese
Chilli Con Carne

BASIC MEAT MIXTURE

ingredients	Metric	Imperial	American
Minced beef	350 g	12 oz	12 oz
Oil	15 ml	1 tbsp	1 tbsp
Onion, peeled and sliced	1	1	1
Tin tomatoes	200 g	7 oz	7 oz
Salt and pepper			

method

1. Heat the oil and fry the onion for 2-3 minutes.

2. Add the minced beef and cook until browned.

3. Add the tomatoes, and season with salt and pepper.

4. Bring to the boil, then reduce the heat, cover, and simmer for 30 minutes.

5. Divide the basic meat mixture into three portions for the following recipes. Two of the portions may be kept in the refrigerator for not more than two days, or (preferably) frozen for later use.

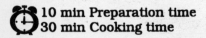 10 min Preparation time
30 min Cooking time

COTTAGE PIE

This is quicker to make if you use instant mashed potato.

ingredients	Metric	Imperial	American
One portion basic meat mixture			
Flour	*12.5 g*	*½ oz*	*½ oz*
Beef stock cube	*½*	*½*	*½*
Hot water	*100 ml*	*4 fl oz*	*½ cup*
Potatoes	*2-3*	*2-3*	*2-3*
Milk	*15 ml*	*1 tbsp*	*1 tbsp*
Butter or margarine	*12.5 g*	*½ oz*	*½ oz*

method

1. Heat the basic meat mixture. Sprinkle over the flour and stir it in.

2. Dissolve the stock cube in the hot water and stir into the meat mixture.

3. Cook the potatoes in boiling, salted water. Mash them with the milk and a little butter.

4. Put the meat mixture into a fireproof dish and then spread the mashed potato over the top. Dot with the remaining butter.

5. Put under a hot grill for 3-4 minutes, until the top is golden brown.

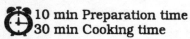 10 min Preparation time
30 min Cooking time

SPAGHETTI BOLOGNESE

ingredients	Metric	Imperial	American
One portion basic meat mixture			
Tomato purée	15 ml	1 tbsp	1 tbsp
Hot water	15 ml	1 tbsp	1 tbsp
Dried herbs	5 ml	1 tsp	1 tsp
Parmesan cheese			

method

1. Heat the basic meat mixture.

2. Mix the tomato purée with the hot water and stir into the meat mixture with the dried herbs.

3. Bring to the boil, then reduce the heat, cover and simmer for 12-15 minutes, while you cook the spaghetti. (See page 75.)

4. Spoon the Bolognese sauce onto the cooked spaghetti and sprinkle generously with Parmesan cheese.

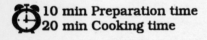 10 min Preparation time
20 min Cooking time

CHILLI CON CARNE

ingredients	Metric	Imperial	American
One portion basic meat mixture			
Chilli powder	5 ml	1 tsp	1 tsp
Tin red kidney beans	200 g	7 oz	7 oz

method

1. Heat the basic meat mixture.

2. Stir in the chilli powder.

3. Drain the red kidney beans, rinse under the tap, and add to the meat mixture.

4. Cover and simmer for 30 minutes.

5. Serve with plain boiled rice, or pitta bread.

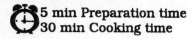
5 min Preparation time
30 min Cooking time

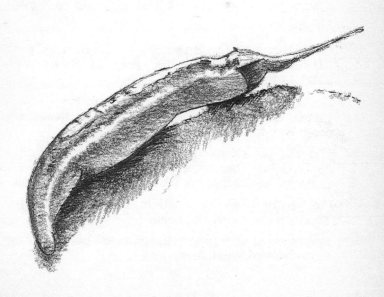

THREE PORK MEALS

Roast Pork with Roast Potatoes
Spicy Pork
Pork and Apple

ROAST PORK WITH ROAST POTATOES

Apple sauce is the traditional accompaniment to roast pork (see page 135).

ingredients	Metric	Imperial	American
Leg of pork	450-675 g	1-1½ lb	1-1½ lb
Potatoes	2-4	2-4	2-4
Cooking fat	25 g	1 oz	1 oz

method

1. Calculate the cooking time - 30 minutes per lb/450 g, plus 30 minutes. Preheat the oven to 375°F/190°C Gas Mark 5.

2. Peel the potatoes and cut them into even-sized pieces. Cook in salted water for 2-3 minutes, then drain into a sieve.

3. Put the pork into an ovenproof dish with the cooking fat. Place in the preheated oven for 5-10 minutes, and when the fat is hot add the potatoes.

4. Continue cooking until meat is tender and potatoes are nicely browned.

5. Eat some of the pork with the roast potatoes and some cooked vegetables.

6.   Leave the rest of the joint to cool. Wrap in clingfilm
      and store in the fridge to use the following day in
      another recipe.

⏰ 20 min Preparation time
   1 - 1¼ hours Cooking time (depending on weight of
   joint)

SPICY PORK

ingredients	Metric	Imperial	American
Cooked pork	*100 g*	*4 oz*	*4 oz*
Salt			
Cayenne pepper			
Butter	*25 g*	*1 oz*	*1 oz*
Worcester sauce	*5 ml*	*1 tsp*	*1 tsp*
Mustard	*2.5 ml*	*½ tsp*	*½ tsp*
Lemon juice	*2.5 ml*	*½ tsp*	*½ tsp*

method

1.   Cut the pork into small pieces and sprinkle with
      salt and a little cayenne.

2.   Melt the butter in a saucepan and add the
      Worcester sauce, mustard and lemon juice. When
      hot, add the meat and toss over the heat for about
      15 minutes, until thoroughly hot and impregnated
      with the flavours.

3.   Serve with rice.

⏰ 20 min Preparation time
   20 min Cooking time

* You can also use leftover cooked pork in a curry. See
the recipe for chicken curry on page 158.

PORK AND APPLE

ingredients	Metric	Imperial	American
Cooked pork	100 g	4 oz	4 oz
Butter	25 g	1 oz	1 oz
Small onion, peeled and finely chopped	1	1	1
Apple, finely chopped	1	1	1
Flour	5 ml	1 tsp	1 tsp
Mustard	pinch	pinch	pinch
Stock	60 ml	4 tbsp	4 tbsp
Salt and pepper			
Lemon juice	2.5 ml	½ tsp	½ tsp

method

1. Cut the cooked meat into neat dice.

2. Melt the butter in a saucepan and cook the onion until soft.

3. Add the apple. Cover and cook until tender.

4. Sprinkle in the flour and mustard. Stir and cook gently for 3 minutes.

5. Add the stock and seasoning. Bring to the boil.

6. Add the meat and lemon juice. Simmer for 25 minutes.

7. Serve with rice or mashed potato.

10 min Preparation time
30 min Cooking time

Two Course Meals
Meals
To Cook in the Oven

When you are cooking for just one person it is not usually economical to use the oven. One small frozen chicken pie in a big hot oven uses a lot of energy! The recipes in this book have been chosen because they can be cooked on top of the stove - except the ones in this section (and also **Three Meals in One**), which have been planned to make good use of the oven once you have turned it on. Each main meal has been paired with a dessert that can be cooked at the same temperature so as to make good use of the oven space.

MENU 1:

Liver and Mushroom Casserole
Jacket Potato
Rice Pudding

Oven temperature: 300°F/150°C Gas Mark 2

ingredients	Metric	Imperial	American
Medium-sized baking potato	1 or 2	1 or 2	1 or 2
For the casserole:			
Lamb's liver	100 g	4 oz	4 oz
Flour	12.5 g	½ oz	½ oz
Salt and pepper			
Small onion, peeled and sliced	1	1	1
Tomato, sliced	1	1	1
Mushrooms, sliced	50 g	2 oz	2 oz
Beef stock	100 ml	4 fl oz	½ cup
For the rice pudding:			
Pudding rice	25 g	1 oz	1 oz
Sugar	12.5 g	½ oz	½ oz
Milk	300 ml	½ pint	1¼ cups

method

1. Preheat the oven to 300°F/150°C Gas Mark 2.

2. Scrub the potato(es) and prick the skin in several places with a fork to prevent bursting during cooking. Rub the skins with a little fat or oil and put them into the oven.

3. Cut the liver into thin slices and toss in flour seasoned with salt and pepper. Arrange a layer of onion in the bottom of a casserole, then the liver, tomato and mushrooms. Pour over the stock and put into the oven.

4. Wash the rice well in cold water and put it into a greased ovenproof dish. Add the sugar and milk. Stir well and put into the oven.

5. After 1¼ hours, test that the potatoes are soft with a skewer. The liver should be tender. The rice pudding should be creamy with a golden brown skin. If necessary, leave to cook for a little longer.

15 min Preparation time
1¼ - 1½ hours Cooking time

MENU 2:

Courgette Bake
Jacket Potato
Baked Apple

Oven temperature: 325°F/160°C Gas Mark 3

ingredients	Metric	Imperial	American
Medium-sized baking potato(es)	1-2	1-2	1-2
For the courgette bake:			
Courgettes, cut into 1 in (2.5 cm) slices	2	2	2
Oil	15 ml	1 tbsp	1 tbsp
Spring onion, finely chopped	1	1	1
Clove of garlic, crushed	1	1	1
Tomatoes, sliced	2-3	2-3	2-3
Cheddar cheese, grated	50 g	2 oz	2 oz
Salt and pepper			
For the baked apple:			
Cooking apple	1	1	1
Dried fruit	25 g	1 oz	1 oz
Brown sugar	5 ml	1 tsp	1 tsp
A knob of butter			

method

1. Preheat the oven to 325°F/160°C Gas Mark 3.

2. Scrub the potato(es) and prick the skin in several places with a fork to prevent bursting during cooking. Rub the skins with a little fat or oil and put them into the oven.

3. Heat the oil in a frying pan and gently fry the sliced courgettes, onion, sliced tomateos and garlic for 10 minutes. Season the mixture with salt and pepper. Spoon into a greased ovenproof dish and sprinkle with cheese. Put into the oven.

4. Remove the core of the apple and score a line round the centre with a knife. Stand the apple in a small ovenproof dish and stuff with the dried fruit and brown sugar. Put a knob of butter on top. Pour a tablespoon of water round the apple and put into the oven.

5   After 50 minutes, test the potatoes and apple with a skewer to see if they are soft. If not, cook for a few minutes longer.

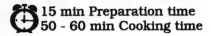 15 min Preparation time
50 - 60 min Cooking time

MENU 3:

Stuffed Pepper
Jacket Potato
Bread and Butter Pudding

Oven temperature: 350°F/180°C Gas Mark 4

ingredients	Metric	Imperial	American
Medium-sized baking potato(es)	*1-2*	*1-2*	*1-2*
For the bread and butter pudding:			
Slices of buttered bread	*2*	*2*	*2*
Currants or sultanas	*25 g*	*1 oz*	*1 oz*
Sugar	*12.5 g*	*½ oz*	*½ oz*
Milk	*225 ml*	*8 fl oz*	*1 cup*
Egg	*1*	*1*	*1*
Ground nutmeg			
For the stuffed pepper:			
Large green pepper	*1*	*1*	*1*
Oil	*15 ml*	*1 tbsp*	*1 tbsp*
Small onion, peeled and sliced	*1*	*1*	*1*
Minced beef	*100 g*	*4 oz*	*4 oz*
Tomato purée	*15 ml*	*1 tbsp*	*1 tbsp*
Cooked rice or breadcrumbs	*1 tbsp*	*1 tbsp*	*1 tbsp*
Mixed dried herbs	*2.5 ml*	*½ tsp*	*½ tsp*
Salt and pepper			
Cheddar cheese, grated	*25 g*	*1 oz*	*1 oz*

method

1. Preheat the oven to 350°F/180°C Gas Mark 4.

2. Scrub the potato(es) and prick the skin in several places with a fork to prevent bursting during cooking. Rub the skins with a little fat or oil and put them into the oven.

3. Cut the bread into squares and arrange in a dish, buttered side up. Sprinkle with dried fruit and sugar. Whisk the milk and eggs together and pour over the bread. Sprinkle with a little nutmeg. Leave to stand while you prepare the stuffed pepper.

4. Cook the pepper in boiling water for 1 minute, then slice off the stalk end and remove the core and seeds. Heat the oil and fry the onion and beef until the meat is brown. Add the other ingredients and mix well. Spoon the mixture into the pepper and stand it in an ovenproof dish. Sprinkle grated cheese on top. Put into the oven with the bread and butter pudding.

5. After 45 minutes, test the potatoes with a skewer to see if they are soft. The cheese on top of the pepper should be brown and bubbly, and the pudding should be lightly browned. Continue cooking for a few more minutes if required.

20 min Preparation time
45 - 60 min Cooking time

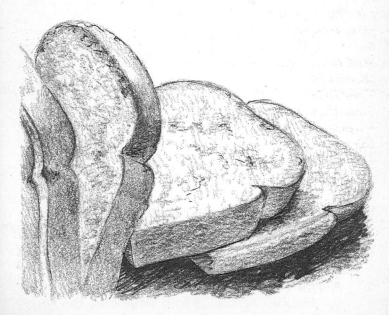

MENU 4:

Chicken Casserole
Scalloped Potatoes
Apple Delight

Oven temperature: 375°F/190°C Gas Mark 5

ingredients	Metric	Imperial	American
For the chicken casserole:			
Chicken joint	1	1	1
Frozen mixed vegetables	50 g	2 oz	2 oz
Tin condensed chicken soup	½	½	½
Salt and pepper			
For the scalloped potatoes:			
Butter			
Large potatoes, peeled and sliced	2	2	2
Small onion, peeled and chopped	1	1	1
Milk	½ cup	½ cup	½ cup
Salt and pepper			
Cheddar cheese, grated	25 g	1 oz	1 oz
For the dessert:			
Cooking apple	1	1	1
Egg	1	1	1
Sugar	50 g	2 oz	2 oz
Flour	25 g	1 oz	1 oz
Milk	300ml	½ pint	1¼ cups
Vanilla essence	2-3 drops	2-3 drops	2-3 drops

method

1. Preheat the oven to 375°F/190°C Gas Mark 5.
2. Put the chicken joint into an ovenproof dish. Add the frozen vegetables and pour over the soup,

undiluted. Season with salt and pepper. Cover with a lid and put into the oven.

3. Smear a little butter round another dish. Arrange the sliced potato in the dish and cover with the onion. Pour over the milk and put a knob of butter on top. Season with salt and pepper and sprinkle on the cheese. Cover with a lid and put into the oven. (Remove the lid 15 minutes before the end of cooking time to allow the top to brown.)

4. Peel, core and cut the apples into wafer-thin slices. Arrange in an ovenproof dish. Whisk the egg with the sugar, then whisk in the flour and milk. Add the vanilla essence and pour over the apples in the pie dish. Put into the oven and cook for 35-40 minutes, until golden brown.

5. Serve the scalloped potatoes with the chicken, followed by the apple delight with cream. (If there is too much dessert for one meal, it is equally nice cold.)

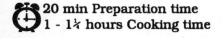 20 min Preparation time
1 - 1¼ hours Cooking time

MENU 5:

Fish Pie
Fruit Crumble

Oven temperature: 375°F/190°C Gas Mark 5

ingredients	Metric	Imperial	American
For the fish pie:			
Fillet of white fish (cod, haddock, etc)	150 g	6 oz	6 oz
Butter	25 g	1 oz	1 oz
Mushrooms, sliced	50 g	2 oz	2 oz
Flour	12.5 g	½ oz	½ oz
Milk (approx)	½ cup	½ cup	½ cup
Tomato, sliced	1	1	1
Cooked, mashed potato (from leftover potatoes, or use instant)	1 cup	1 cup	1 cup
For the fruit crumble:			
Apple, plums, rhubarb, etc	150 g	6 oz	6 oz
Sugar	50 g	2 oz	2 oz
Flour	50 g	2 oz	2 oz
Margarine	25 g	1 oz	1 oz

method

1. Preheat the oven to 375°F/190°C Gas Mark 5.

2. Poach the fish in a little water until it flakes. Melt the butter in a saucepan and fry the mushrooms for 3-4 minutes. Stir in the flour and cook for another minute. Strain the water in which the fish was cooked into a cup and add milk to make a full cup. Stir into the saucepan and bring to the boil. Add the flaked fish and season with salt and pepper. Spoon into an ovenproof dish and cover with sliced tomato, then the mashed potato. Dot the top with butter and put into the oven.

3. Prepare the fruit and put into a small ovenproof dish. Sprinkle over half the sugar. Put the remaining sugar, flour and margarine into a basin and rub with the fingertips until the mixture resembles breadcrumbs. Spread the crumble over the fruit and put into the oven.

4. After 30 minutes, check that both the fish pie and fruit crumble are nicely browned. If not, cook a little longer.

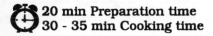 20 min Preparation time
30 - 35 min Cooking time

MENU 6:

Chinese Pork
Oven Chips
Mincemeat or Jam Turnovers

Oven temperature: 400°F/200°C Gas Mark 6

ingredients	Metric	Imperial	American
Oven chips			
For the Chinese pork:			
Pork chop	*1*	*1*	*1*
Hoisin sauce	*30 ml*	*2 tbsp*	*2 tbsp*
Soy sauce	*15 ml*	*1 tbsp*	*1 tbsp*
Sherry	*15 ml*	*1 tbsp*	*1 tbsp*
For the turnovers:			
Ready-made flaky or rough puff pastry	*75 g*	*3 oz*	*3 oz*
Jam or mincemeat			

method

1. In a small basin mix together the hoisin sauce, soy sauce and sherry. Put the chop into an ovenproof dish and spread the marinade sauce all over it. Leave to marinate for an hour.

2. Preheat the oven to 400°F/200°C Gas Mark 6.

3. When the oven is hot, put in the oven chips and pork chop.

4. Roll out the pastry and cut it into two squares. Put a spoonful of jam or mincemeat into the centre, dampen the edges and fold the pastry over to form a triangle. Brush with milk and make a small slit in the top of each. Put on a greased baking tin and bake in the oven until golden brown. Sprinkle with sugar before eating.

5. Make a salad to eat with the chips and pork chop.

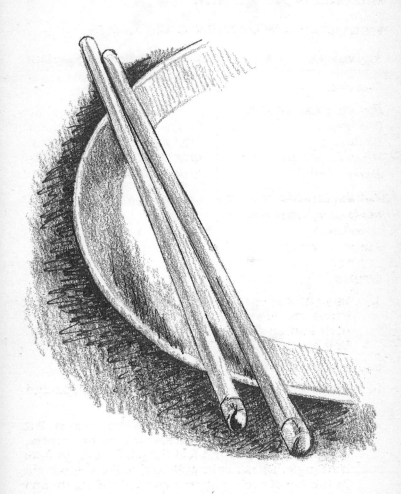

15 min Preparation time
(plus 1 hour marinating time)
35 - 40 min Cooking time

VEGETABLE Dishes

More and more people are recognising the importance of vegetables in our diet, as they provide fibre and vitamin C. Make sure you buy vegetables that are really fresh, and use them quickly otherwise much of their goodness is lost. Frozen are a better bet than something you have kept in the vegetable rack for a couple of weeks. They also have the advantage of being ready-prepared. You don't have to be a vegetarian to enjoy the dishes below.

CAULIFLOWER, POTATO AND PEA CURRY

Eat this delicious vegetable curry with brown rice (see page 106-107) or naan bread.

ingredients	Metric	Imperial	American
Cauliflower florets	*100 g*	*4 oz*	*4 oz*
Potato, peeled and cut into chunks	*1*	*1*	*1*
Vegetable oil	*45 ml*	*3 tbsp*	*3 tbsp*
Cumin seeds	*1 ml*	*¼ tsp*	*¼ tsp*
Green chilli	*1*	*1*	*1*
Fresh grated ginger	*1 ml*	*¼ tsp*	*¼ tsp*
Ground cumin	*2.5 ml*	*½ tsp*	*½ tsp*
Turmeric powder	*2.5 ml*	*½ tsp*	*½ tsp*
Salt			
Water	*110 ml*	*4 fl oz*	*½ cup*
Peas (fresh or frozen)	*50 g*	*2 oz*	*2 oz*

method

1. Heat the oil and fry the cauliflower and potato until lightly brown.

2. Add the cumin seeds and fry for 1 minute.

3. Add the green chilli, grated ginger, ground cumin, turmeric and salt. Stir well and fry for another minute.

4. Add the water, and when it is boiling add the peas.

5. Cover and simmer for 8 minutes, until the cauliflower and potato are tender.

6. Serve with brown rice or naan bread.

⏰ 10 min Preparation time
15 min Cooking time

Aubergine with Bulgur Wheat

ingredients	Metric	Imperial	American
Small aubergine	1	1	1
Salt			
Bulgur wheat	½ cup	½ cup	½ cup
Water	1 cup	1 cup	1 cup
Olive oil	30 ml	2 tbsp	2 tbsp
Small onion, peeled and sliced	1	1	1
Ground cumin	5 ml	1 tsp	1 tsp
Ground coriander	5 ml	1 tsp	1 tsp
Raisins	25 g	1 oz	1 oz
Flaked almonds	25 g	1 oz	1oz
Black pepper			

method

1. Chop the aubergine into small cubes. Sprinkle with salt and leave for 15 minutes.

2. Put the bulgur wheat and water into a saucepan, bring to the boil and then reduce the heat and simmer for 10 minutes, or until all the water is absorbed.

3. Meanwhile heat the olive oil and cook the onion until soft.

4. Add the aubergine and stir-fry until lightly brown.

5. Add the cumin, coriander, raisins and almonds. Cook for another minute.

6. Stir in the bulgur wheat and season with plenty of black pepper.

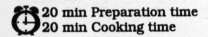
20 min Preparation time
20 min Cooking time

COLCANNON

This traditional Irish dish is a meal in itself – or non-vegetarians may like to eat it with some ham.

ingredients	Metric	Imperial	American
Potatoes	150 g	6 oz	6 oz
Cabbage	150 g	6 oz	6 oz
Spring onions	3	3	3
Milk	5o ml	2 fl oz	¼ cup
Grated nutmeg			
Knob of butter			
Salt and pepper			

method

1. Peel the potatoes, cut into chunks and cook in boiling water until soft. Drain and mash.

2. Finely shred the cabbage and cook in boiling water until soft.

3. Meanwhile chop the spring onions and simmer them in the milk, with a pinch of nutmeg, for 5 minutes.

4. Mix the cooked cabbage into the mashed potatoes, and stir in the milk, spring onions, and a knob of butter. Season well with salt and pepper.

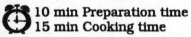
10 min Preparation time
15 min Cooking time

PEPERONATA

This dish tastes even better when reheated, So it is
worth making double the quantity and saving half for
another meal. You can use different coloured peppers,
or only red ones. Sweet peppers are a good source of
vitamin C, and the red and yellow ones also contain
vitamin A. Eat the peperonata with any variety of
pasta, preferably wholemeal.

ingredients	Metric	Imperial	American
Small red pepper	1	1	1
Small yellow pepper	1	1	1
Small green pepper	1	1	1
Olive oil	5 ml	1 tbsp	1 tbsp
Small onion, peeled and sliced	1	1	1
Clove of garlic, crushed	1	1	1
Tomatoes, peeled and chopped	2	2	2
Basil leaves, chopped (optional)	3-4	3-4	3-4
Salt			

method

1. Remove the stalks, seeds and white membrane
   and cut the peppers into strips.

2. Heat the oil and cook the onion and garlic until
   lightly browned.

3. Add the peppers. Cover and cook for 15 minutes.

4. Add the tomatoes, basil leaves and salt. Cook for
   another 15 minutes.

5. Serve with pasta.

10 min Preparation time
35 min Cooking time

RATATOUILLE WITH PASTA

This is particularly nice if you use wholewheat pasta.

ingredients	Metric	Imperial	American
Pasta shapes	75-100 g	3-4 oz	3-4 oz
Small aubergine	1	1	1
Courgette	1	1	1
Olive or sunflower oil	15 ml	1 tbsp	1 tbsp
Small onion, sliced	1	1	1
Clove of garlic, crushed	1	1	1
Green or red pepper	½	½	½
Tin tomatoes	200 g	7 oz	7 oz
Dried herbs	2.5 ml	½ tsp	½ tsp
Salt and pepper			

method

1. Cut the aubergine and courgette into finger shapes about 1 cm/½ in thick. Put into a sieve and sprinkle with salt. Leave to drain for 10 minutes, then pat dry with kitchen paper.

2. Meanwhile cook the pasta and drain it.

3. Heat the oil in a saucepan and add the onion and garlic. Fry gently for 3 minutes.

4. Add the pepper, aubergine and courgette and cook for another 3 minutes.

5. Add the tomatoes and herbs. Season with salt and pepper and cook for another 3 minutes.

6. Stir in the cooked pasta, and heat through for 1 minute before eating.

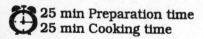 25 min Preparation time
25 min Cooking time

MUSHROOM CURRY

ingredients	Metric	Imperial	American
Vegetable oil	15 ml	1 tbsp	1 tbsp
Knob of butter			
Potato, peeled and diced	1	1	1
Small onion, peeled and chopped	1	1	1
Clove of garlic, crushed	1	1	1
Fresh grated ginger	2·5 ml	½ tsp	½ tsp
Ground cumin	2·5 ml	½ tsp	½ tsp
Ground coriander	2·5 ml	½ tsp	½ tsp
Turmeric	2·5 ml	½ tsp	½ tsp
Button mushrooms	150 g	6 oz	6 oz
Tomatoes, skinned and chopped	2	2	2
Natural yoghurt	15 ml	1 tbsp	1 tbsp
Lemon juice	5 ml	1 tsp	1 tsp
Salt and pepper			

method

1. Heat the oil and butter in a saucepan and fry the potato and onion for 4-5 minutes.

2. Add the garlic, ginger and spices and cook for another minute.

3. Add the mushrooms, tomatoes, yoghurt and lemon juice. Season well with salt and pepper.

4. Serve with brown rice.

🕐 10 min Preparation time
30 min Cooking time

INDEX